E-Business Basics for Law Firms

Related titles by Law Society Publishing

The Internet
Andrew Terrett

Internet Marketing
Edited by Nicola Webb

Legal Technology
Charles Christian

Managing Cyber-Risks
Rupert Kendrick

Marketing, Management and Motivation
Dianne Bown-Wilson and Gail Courtney

Marketing Your Law Firm (includes CD)
Lucy Adam

Titles from Law Society Publishing can be ordered from all good legal bookshops or direct from our distributors, Marston Book Services (telephone 01235 465656 or e-mail *law.society@ marston.co.uk*). For further information or a catalogue call our editorial and marketing office on 020 7320 5878.

E-Business Basics for Law Firms

Christina Archbold

The Law Society

ISBN 1–85328–752–0

Published in 2003 by the Law Society
113 Chancery Lane, London WC2A 1PL

Typeset by J&L Composition, Filey, North Yorkshire
Printed by Antony Rowe Ltd, Chippenham, Wilts

Definitions of e-business (p.1), portals (p.102–3) and virus (p.26) copyrighted by and used with permission of whatis.com and TechTarget Inc.

05284722

Contents

List of abbreviations

ADSL	Asymmetric Digital Subscriber Loop
ASP	1. Active Server Pages
	2. Application Service Provision
ATM	Automatic Teller Machine
B2B	Business to Business
B2C	Business to Consumer
C2B	Consumer to Business
C2C	Consumer to Consumer
CA	Certification Authority
CBI	Confederation of British Industry
CBT	Computer based training
CD	Compact Disc
CGI	Common Gateway Interface
CRM	Client Relationship Management
DIY	Do It Yourself
EDI	Electronic Data Interchange
EFT	Electronic Funds Transfer
EIP	Enterprise Information Portal
FTP	File Transfer Protocol
GIF	Graphics Interchange Format
GPRS	General Packet Radio Service
HTML	HyperText Markup Language
HTTP	Hypertext Transfer Protocol
IP	Internet Protocol
IPO	Initial Public Offering
ISDN	Integrated Services Digital Network
ISP	Internet Service Provider
IT	Information Technology
ITT	Invitation To Tender
JPEG	Joint Photographics Experts Group
LSC	Legal Services Commission
MIME	Multi-purpose Internet Mail Extensions
Mbps	Megabytes per second
PC	Personal Computer
PDA	Personal Digital Assistant

PKI	Public Key Infrastructure
RAM	Random Access Memory
RFI	Request For Information
SCM	Supply Chain Management
SWOT	Strengths, Weaknesses, Opportunities and Threats
TTP	Trusted Third Party
URL	Universal Resource Locator
VPN	Virtual Private Network
W3C	World Wide Web Consortium
WAI	Web Accessibility Initiative
WP	Word Processing
WWW	World Wide Web (the web)
XML	eXtended Markup Language

Acknowledgements

Since joining the Law Society in 1994 it has been my privilege to have a unique viewpoint of the legal IT world and I would sincerely like to acknowledge the contribution of colleagues and friends past and present at the Law Society. In particular I'd like to thank John Miller and Sue Cummings for their ongoing personal support and their undaunted commitment to helping solicitors with IT. Thanks too to Maureen Miller, Morag Goldfinch, Paula Crowhurst and Neil Gower who have all provided a great sounding board over the years as well as Robin ap Cynan, Tony Fisher, Simon Young, David Cannell and Neil Davidson who have all provided a great deal of food for thought and practical insight.

I would also like to thank Jane Withey, my editor, whose patience and encouragement throughout the arduous process of writing has been little short of saintly.

A big thank you too to Nicki Tanner and Alison Brooks at SKAI for their continuous encouragement and to all at Landmark Education – in particular Imran Shah and Helga Christian – for their unfailing stand for what is possible in my life and the life of others.

Finally, heartfelt thanks to Liz Dean, good friend and fellow trumpet player for patiently editing and collating the manuscript and keeping me going when I just wanted to give up, and to the boys in my band Blue Soup (Graham, Mike and Kostas) for giving me something else to think about from time to time! Thanks would also not be complete without recognising the great support and dear friendship of Gary Day and Andrew Williamson both of whom are sadly missed.

And last but certainly not least, huge heartfelt thanks to my Mum, whose practical support was the biggest contribution of all. Thanks Mum.

Christina Archbold
April 2003

Introduction

It suddenly seems that 'e' is everywhere, attaching itself to the front of once ordinary words. There is e-mail, e-zine, e-insurance, e-commerce, e-gaming, e-tail, and now the 'e' has landed in the legal world with e-conveyancing.

So what's all the fuss about? What does e-business actually mean and what is its relevance to law firms? And having made sense of this should you get involved and if so how? These are some of the questions that this book will answer. It is designed to be a beginner's practical guide offering some ideas to get you started. It won't give you all the answers, as e-business is a huge field of endeavour, but it seeks to set you thinking in a useful direction.

So is this another book about the Internet? Yes and no. The approach taken here is different in that the primary focus is on legal business first and foremost. The main thrust is incorporating the benefits and advantages of the Internet into the day-to-day working of a firm. Put another way, it is about web-enabling legal practice, or incorporating the Internet into legal business processes. More fundamentally though, it is about transforming client care and service through the use of Internet technologies and the World Wide Web.

The speed of change

The speed of change is a new phenomenon. In 1999, traffic on the Internet was estimated to be doubling every hundred days. Putting this in perspective, the Internet took four years to reach 50 million users, compared with 16 years for personal computers, 13 years for television and 38 years for radio. It is said that change on the Internet happens at seven times the normal rate as in the 'real' world.

Growth and size of the Internet

The phenomenal growth of the Internet measured in physical terms such as the number of computers attached, the number of websites and the number of users is very impressive – from a handful of computers connected from 1958 to 1992 to an incredible explosion by 1993 to 10 million growing to 950 million in 2000. Today that figure is well over 100 million. That's a lot of computers!

Business on the Internet

The history of the first speculative boom and bust that happened amid the frenzy of dot.com IPOs (initial public offerings) also provides an interesting perspective on where the Internet is going. The whole story is entertainingly told by John Cassidy in *Dot.Con*.[1] The book is about speculative bubbles in general and the Internet speculative bubble in particular. Interestingly it seems most great inventions that were to fundamentally change the way we live were subject to initial speculative booms and busts, railways and electricity amongst them. Maybe the lesson to be learnt (if there is one) is that the Internet is going through the growing pains of all great inventions that eventually have a significant impact on our lives. In many ways we are like eighteenth-century farmers wondering about the impact of steam, or the Victorians speculating about electricity and the railways.

Why this book now?

If there is one myth that everyone agrees on about law firms, it is that they don't like change; the tired old jokes about quill pens still abound. After all, the business of law has been around for a good few hundred years and has survived quite happily all previous inventions, including electricity, the telephone, photocopier, fax and word processor. The death knell for the high street firm has been sounded many times, yet many small firms still thrive and prosper. So what, if anything, is different this time?

Two things. The first is the speed of change – there is now very little time to sit back for a few years and see what happens, there is a risk of being left behind. The other is that this particular set of new technologies is about mass and instant dissemination of information – the stock in trade of the lawyer – and is directly applicable to business, with the potential to change the nature of business itself.

Also, of course, law firms don't operate in a vacuum and the Internet is having an effect on the daily life of the majority of the western world. It is insidious: last year it was normal to book your airline tickets over the phone, this year you automatically do it on the web. It's normal to start a conversation about insurance on the phone and finish off the paperwork on a website. Finding your way around a new city? You look up the street map on the web. Want to check your bank balance? You do it on the web. Want the latest news? You check out bbc.co.uk. And then there is e-mail and webcams and instant messaging. Mobile phones are evolving into mini-supercomputers; e-mail and Internet surfing is on the move. Text messaging has gone crazy, and nobody predicted that. We're all adopting new technologies at an unprecedented pace and with it our expectations of how and when things should get done is being revolutionised.

Time now really is of the essence. The message of this book is it is time to start thinking and implementing the 'e' in the business of law.

CASE STUDY   **How the West was Won – a comparative fable**

In many ways the colonisation of cyberspace has been very similar to the colonisation of the Wild West. First come the prospectors, who find gold. The word gets out and increasing numbers turn up to make their fortune. After a while, canny people spot that the way to make money is not to do the prospecting, but to provide the infrastructure for the gold-diggers, selling food, spades and all the other necessary items needed for survival. It's not long before the desire for entertainment is exploited with saloons and other forms of adult entertainment. Then as things start to get unruly law enforcement arrives and when that creates some certainty, settlers find their way and a small town springs up. People start to trade using money instead of gold or barter and banks and other financial institutions open. Then the gold runs out and there is a crisis; however, a local economy has developed sufficiently alongside the xiv Introduction

prospecting that people carry on regardless. Then come the railroad and the telegraph office and before long people are arriving to take advantage of the cheap land and employment opportunities provided by a new and vibrant community. Next come churches, schools and hospitals; the settlement becomes a city with a university, a city hall and full blown self-sustaining economy complete with its own transport and telecommunications infrastructure. Welcome to San Francisco! (which, by the way, happens to be a stone's throw from Silicon Valley).

In terms of Internet development and where we are today, the sheriff has just shown up and is busy trying to bring some law and order to the unruly inhabitants. Serious work has begun on authentication and digital signatures to bring some order to the confusion of online trading, and in the wake of September 11 there is an ongoing debate about governments being able to secretly monitor web activity. The railway has been promised and is on its way to everyone some time soon (broadband). The speculative boom has come to an end (the dot.com crash) and people are now looking at how to develop and grow normal business. Now it is time for the lawyers . . .

Note

1   Cassidy, John (2002) *Dot.Con: The greatest story ever sold*, Penguin, London.

1

What is e-business?

> We are on the verge of a revolution that is just as profound as the change in the economy that came with the Industrial Revolution. Soon electronic networks will allow people to transcend the barriers of time and distance and take advantage of global markets and business opportunities not even imaginable today, opening up a new world of economic possibility and progress.
>
> Albert Gore, Jr., Former US Vice-President

What is e-business?

A simple definition for e-business is:

> The conduct of business on the Internet, not only buying and selling but also servicing customers and collaborating with business partners.
>
> **whatis.com**

The term e-business is sometimes used interchangeably with e-commerce. In this book the term will be used to mean the broader concept of using the Internet as a primary or complementary means of developing and delivering services.

E-business can be classified into four main types according to the type of user and provider in the transaction. This is illustrated in Figure 1.1

- *Business-to-business (B2B)*. Although less well publicised, B2B businesses generate far larger revenues than B2C. Examples are services such as Blue Flag for corporate clients and legal publishers' online services.
- *Business-to-consumer (B2C)*. These types of e-business fared worst in the dot.com crash and as a result have been the most publicised; they are usually online stores or shopping sites. Examples include online retailers such as Amazon.co.uk and direct sales companies such as Dell.com.

	USER	
	Business	Consumer
PROVIDER Business	B2B	B2C
Consumer	C2B	C2C

Figure 1.1 Types of e-business

- *Consumer-to-consumer (C2C).* This is one of the fastest growing sectors and one where the Internet provides significant advantages over normal channels. Examples include classified advertising sites such as loot.com that allow people to post adverts, and auction sites such as e-Bay.com that allow people to put items up for auction and take bids.
- *Consumer-to-Business (C2B).* This category includes individuals who offer their services to businesses, such as freelance computer programmers.

What is e-commerce?

E-commerce is a subset of e-business and refers to the process of buying and selling online. It can be taken to include all financial and commercial transactions that take place electronically, including electronic data interchange (EDI) and electronic funds transfer (EFT), and all credit/debit card activity. These activities have been around far longer than the Internet using proprietary electronic networks. Alternatively it can be understood simply as retail sales over the Internet.

E-commerce is something that many law firms have felt is not relevant to them since it has been hard to envisage how legal advice, which by its very definition is bespoke, can be sold online. What law firms are doing around the buying and selling of legal services will be covered in Chapter 3.

Clicks 'n' mortar

This is a term that is often used to describe a traditional business that exists in the real world, that is with premises, that also makes use of the Internet in its operations. This term covers the vast majority of businesses online today including most of the law firms that will be discussed in Chapter 3.

E-business versus having a website

Clearly, e-business as described above could not exist without the Internet. However, it is useful not to confuse the message with the medium. The Internet is the medium by which electronic goods and services can be delivered and in essence it forms another channel or route to market for businesses.

Having a website does not necessarily mean you are in e-business, rather it is the intention of the website that makes the difference. For example, a brochureware website may help attract business to your firm, but your firm may not be involved in e-business. If your firm were to use the same website to attract trade, and then service some part of that trade, then you are in e-business. In essence, e-business is where some or all of a business process is undertaken online.

The impact of e-business

Despite the recent downturn in dot.com company fortunes, e-business is growing rapidly. More and more companies and institutions are investing in the Internet as a viable alternative channel to deliver products and services to their customers.

> Global electronic commerce revenue for 2000 was in the region of $286 billion; a figure which was expected to increase to $500 billion this year and to exceed $3 trillion in 2004.
>
> The Law Commission, *Electronic Commerce:*
> *Formal Requirements in Commercial Transactions,*
> December 2001, **www.lawcom.gov.uk**

What do law firms think of e-business?

In recent independent market research conducted by the Law Society,[1] law firms were asked their opinions on the impact of e-business. The results showed a limited general understanding and awareness:

- It's irrelevant (26 per cent).
- It won't have a dramatic effect (18 per cent).
- We have no idea (17 per cent).
- We expect an increase in business (10 per cent).
- There will be a greater use of e-mail (4 per cent).
- We recognise the need to use e-commerce in business (3 per cent).
- There will be an increase in use (2 per cent).
- Changes in conveyancing law will affect usage (2 per cent).
- We'll update our website to make more use of it (2 per cent).
- We plan to use it for conveyancing, quotes, etc. (2 per cent).
- Clients will want to access files, they will want online reporting (2 per cent).
- It will mean a greater use of the Internet (1 per cent).
- It increases the speed of communication (1 per cent).

Further independent market research conducted in 2003 by The Law Society[2] showed that the Internet services used and being considered were as follows:

- e-mail (97 per cent);
- research/information (91 per cent);
- downloading forms (79 per cent);
- own website (64 per cent);
- intranet connection (42 per cent);
- considering e-conveyancing (41 per cent);
- planning a website (21 per cent);
- considering an intranet (14 per cent);
- Land Registry online (2 per cent);
- online banking (1 per cent);
- online buying (1 per cent).

The samples were drawn from law firms who were already active in the IT arena having installed fully integrated practice management software. Overall it appears there is limited understanding and take up of the opportunities that e-business has to offer.

It is interesting to contrast this with other statistics described below.[3]

UK demographics

- Over 50 per cent of the total UK population have accessed the Internet on one or more occasions over the past 12 months.
- Seventy per cent of all Internet users are over the age of 24 and 71 per cent fall into the social group categories ABC1s.
- An estimated 50 per cent of the UK's online population earn more than £25,000 p.a.

In other words, the people using the Internet are precisely the people that law firms want to attract as clients.

Legal market usage

- Three thousand firms have launched websites, that is approximately one third of the law firms in England and Wales.
- Eighty per cent of these are 'brochureware'.
- Twenty-five per cent offer some kind of quotation facility (e.g. for conveyancing).
- Six per cent have some 'e-commerce' element.
- Three per cent offer extranet facilities enabling clients and other interested parties to access matter information via the web.

E-mail usage

- In the UK 360 million e-mails are sent and received *every day*.
- E-mail usage has increased over 600 per cent in the past five years.
- Forty per cent of lawyers with Internet access receive more than 40 e-mails a day.

- Sixty per cent of lawyers leave their e-mails to be dealt with by their secretarial and support staff.
- Seventy-seven per cent of all lawyers now have Internet access (ranging from 60 per cent among sole practitioners to 90 per cent in larger firms).
- Ten per cent of lawyers with Internet access have never used it in practice.

Online legal service usage

It is estimated that 2 per cent of all undefended divorce proceedings are now commenced online, typically via a non-law firm online legal service.

The relevance of e-business

Being a knowledge-based business providing professional advice and services to clients within a strict code of professional conduct means that the relevance of e-business to law firms may not be instantly apparent. However, there are drivers to action that are relevant to all businesses, be they professional service firms or manufacturing companies. These are summarised in Table 1.1.

Table 1.1 Drivers to action for the legal business

Driver	Legal business ideas
Increasing speed with which supplies can be obtained	Online interaction with legal agencies (e.g. Land Registry, Companies House, Legal Services Commission, etc.) Ordering of supplies, e.g. stationery Online legal research information
Increasing speed with which goods can be despatched	Quicker interaction with clients (via e-mail and possibly a client extranet)
Reduced sales and purchasing costs	Ability to shop around online for best deals Ability to club together with other firms to reduce costs (see Virtual Solicitors Chambers) Reduced paper costs (maybe!) Less time spent on legal research

Table 1.1 (*continued*)

Driver	Legal business ideas
Reduced operating costs	Reduced administration costs by automating leave forms, etc. using an intranet Cheaper online recruitment Invoice payment Electronic banking
Customer demand	Clients (particularly commercial clients) becoming 'net savvy' and expecting more to be delivered online as they see potential cost savings
Improving the range and quality of services offered	Ability to develop 'value webs' (see Chapter 3) and offer more service around the total client experience (e.g. a house moving service rather than a conveyancing service)
Avoiding losing market share to businesses already using e-commerce	Avoiding competitive disadvantage from other firms who are already getting into online transaction mode

Notes

1 Research undertaken by Moulton Hall Ltd, 2001.
2 Research undertaken by The Business Research Unit, 2003.
3 Source: Christian, Charles (2002) *On-line Strategies for Smaller Law Firms* **www.legaltechnology.com**.

Getting started

Everything you need to know about e-business technology but were afraid to ask

> On two occasions I have been asked [by members of Parliament], 'Pray, Mr Babbage, if you put into the machine wrong figures, will the right answers come out?' I am not able rightly to apprehend the kind of confusion of ideas that could provoke such a question.
>
> Charles Babbage, 'Father of Computing'

The Internet is an increasingly complex set of technologies. This chapter is a brief explanation of the 'plumbing' of the Internet, explaining some of the more important technologies and concepts.

What exactly is the Internet and how does it work?

When most people talk about the Internet, they usually mean the World Wide Web and e-mail. The World Wide Web (WWW or simply the web) is simply a network of computers (web servers) that are all connected and allow people to access (browse) the information (websites) stored on them. Anyone (with a little money) can develop a website and make it available to the world at large. And in a way this is all you need to know. The far more interesting question is what does this make available to the legal business and in particular your business?

However, some people like to know a little of what's under the bonnet so what follows is a simple explanation of the technologies. There are some very interesting aspects to the way in which the web works which are at the heart of what it is and what makes it different from previous technologies that have come our way.

A quick look at the plumbing of the Internet

Internet infrastructure

The Internet is actually a network of computer networks, which are physically separate and linked together only at very specific points. Every network that wants to be on the Internet needs to use a set of 'communication protocols' known as the Internet Protocols (IP).

Each network has its own network operating software and the most popular ones used on the Internet are Windows NT (from Microsoft) and Linux. There is a hot debate about which is the better system, which tends to focus on the fact that Microsoft is a commercial company making money, whilst Linux is offered virtually free of charge over the Internet. This does not really affect you, unless you decide to build your own website using a web development package. It then becomes important to know which operating system your hosting company is using on its web servers. As it is likely that you will be getting expert help on building your website and an Internet Service Provider (ISP) to host it, how this actually works in practice may be of little concern. There will be more about Internet Service Providers later.

How information travels across the Internet

When you send an e-mail across the Internet or visit a website the information appears to travel almost instantaneously to its destination. However, all is not what it seems!

One of the key things that the designers of the Internet were keen to have happen (given that it was originally designed to be a network that could survive a nuclear attack) was that communication would still be possible, even if portions of the network ceased to exist. To enable this they designed a way of sending information which involves breaking it up into 'packets' and routing them across the network in different directions. Each packet knows its final destination and, once all the packets arrive, they are reassembled instantaneously into the whole message.

Table 2.1 summarises the key components of the Internet which we will be looking at in further detail.

Table 2.1 Key components of the Internet

Component/technology	Function
Hypertext	A way of linking one piece of text to another piece of text, enabling you to access it through simply clicking on the link. Text that has an associated link is usually blue and underlined
Web server	The computer on which websites are hosted and which is linked to the Internet
Website	A collection of information pages (called web pages) structured in a way that is navigable via hypertext links. The first page you see is called the home page
Communications links	Telephone lines. These can provide Internet access at various speeds
Web browser	The piece of software that you use to browse the web. See also Table 2.2.

Hypertext and multimedia

Hypertext is so much part of the normal web landscape that now we no longer even think about it. However, the idea that you can reference a piece of information from any other piece of information simply by clicking on a 'link' is revolutionary. What is even more extraordinary is that the link can be to any piece of any information anywhere on the web. This is what gives the 'web' its name – it is literally billions of pages of information that are linked and interlinked in a multifaceted web.

In reality, while the capability to link across the globe is undoubtedly useful, the truly useful aspect is using the capability to manage and access your own information internally (using an intranet) and to a limited number of external interested parties, e.g. clients and counsel (using client extranets and virtual deal rooms). There is more about intranets and extranets later in the chapter.

The other characteristic of web pages is that they can be multimedia, that is they can contain not only text, but also images, video and sound. It is also possible to stream TV, radio and music over the Internet in 'real' time.

E-mail

Most law firms are now using some form of e-mail to communicate both internally and with the external world. This too has revolutionised the way in which communication happens. There are still issues of authentication to be tackled to enable it to become the primary medium of communication in business, but most routine communication now takes place by e-mail and telephone.

How e-mail works

At the simplest level, e-mail works in a rather similar fashion to ordinary mail (or snail mail as it is called on the Internet). You type the address of the recipient (which is usually some variant of their name plus their website address, or ISP provider, e.g. **name@domainname.co.uk** or **name@ISPname.com**) at the top of the message together with the e-mail addresses of the people you want the message to be copied to, if any. Once the message is ready to go, hitting the send button will transmit it from your computer to your ISP's mail server. From your ISP it will then be forwarded to the ISP of the recipient of your e-mail. It will then be sent directly to the receipient's network and desktop, if they have this facility, or sit in the equivalent of a mailbox until they next collect (download) their e-mail.

A useful feature of e-mail is the ability to be able to attach files, i.e. Word documents, Excel spreadsheets, video files, etc. to the message. This has the message act more like an envelope for the file.

FTP

FTP stands for File Transfer Protocol and is really a way of moving large files of information from one server to another. In a way it's like taking a large matter file from one filing cabinet and putting it in another. The most common use for FTP is to transfer files from the computer that has been used to develop a website to the web server where it will be made available on the Internet.

Why are web technologies different and why use them?

The key thing about web technologies is that they are cheap and easy to use. Web browsers come free of charge and linking to the

Internet is relatively cheap. Simple websites cost hundreds rather than thousands of pounds and e-mails cost pence.

Table 2.2 describes typical applications (products and tools used to perform specific tasks) used on the Internet.

Table 2.2 Typical applications on the Internet

Application	Function	Product used
E-mail	See the text for a description	See the accompanying text
Web browsers	Used to access the WWW and visit websites or run browser-based applications	Browser software from Microsoft (Internet Explorer) or Netscape (Netscape Navigator)
FTP (File Transfer Protocol)	Provides a way to upload and download information and software to and from websites. Can be public or private access	FTP transfer software programs. A host of these are available virtually free of charge on the web
Newsgroups	Technically separate from the WWW, these provide discussion groups on an amazingly wide range of topics including law	Most browsers support newsgroup functions
Chat and instant messaging	Interactive (almost) discussion groups with members preselecting themselves	Microsoft instant messenger, Netscape AOL, ICQ, service specific chat rooms
Conferencing	Various methods are used to communicate with others over the Internet, including voice, video and data conferencing	Many products, including Microsoft NetMeeting. ISPs also tend to offer this as part of a hosting package if required
Mail list servers	Allow bulk e-mail delivery to a selected group of people	Offered by most ISPs. Can be purchased as software products, and websites such as Yahoo! provide group functions where members subscribe and receive all postings of e-mail
Video clips	Provide a method of delivering real-time video to the desktop (if you have sufficient bandwidth)	Microsoft, Apple and Real Networks provide media players

Table 2.2 (*continued*)

Application	Function	Product used
TV and radio streaming	Satellite TV and live radio broadcasting over the Internet usually at the same time as the real broadcast, again dependent on bandwidth	Microsoft, Apple and Real Networks media players are used to stream this to the desktop

What's a domain name?

The Internet is a series of computers linked together for the purpose of making information available to the world. How does this work?

Each computer that is connected to the Internet (or more accurately to a web server) has its own unique IP (Internet Protocol) address. This is an identification number for the physical machine that allows it to be found on the Internet. This works in conjunction with a system of universal resource locators (URLs) also known as web addresses or domain names which we are all familiar with. A typical domain name is **www.lawsociety.org.uk**.

Domain names allow you to register a name that is meaningful for your firm (e.g. **www.lawfirm.co.uk**). Rather like registering company names, each domain name has to be unique and rules are emerging which prevent people from 'squatting' domain names simply for the purpose of making money out of individuals and companies who could legitimately want to use that name.

Each domain name has an extension (e.g. .com or .co.uk), which usually describes the function of the organisation that holds the domain name. Table 2.3 lists the most popular extensions. This area is growing rapidly and new extensions are being developed all the time.

It is very important to register a domain name for your firm that will make sense to the potential users of your website. Unfortunately at this stage of the game, most of the easy to remember legal style domain names (such as law.com, lawyers. co.uk and so on) have been registered. Now the game is to find a domain name that is meaningful and useful!

Table 2.3 Domain name extensions

Extension	Used for
.com	Commercial organisation
.co	A company
.org	A not for profit organisation
.ac	An academic institution
.info	A general 'information provider' extension
.biz	A business
.co.uk	A company registered in the UK
.org.au	A not for profit organisation in Australia
.co.ie	A company in Ireland
.pro	An extension that is currently being developed for professionals (see **www.registrypro.com**)
.gov	Government websites

How do you access the Internet?

Internet Service Providers

To gain access to the Internet backbone, which is like the main highway of the Internet, most organisations and individuals use an intermediary called an Internet Service Provider (ISP). For a small subscription, you dial into your ISP's web server and this gives you access to the Internet. From the user perspective this is an invisible process and to all intents and purposes once you have dialled up you are 'out' on the Internet free to go where you please.

It is possible to purchase your own access directly to the Internet, but for many reasons, not least expense and the hassle of managing what is a complex infrastructure, most organisations choose to use an ISP.

ISPs, as well as providing access to the Internet, also provide e-mail services and host websites. Hosting means putting a website on a web server and making it accessible on the Internet. When the web first entered popular commercial consciousness (around 1995) most companies hosted their own web server, that is they bought another computer and connected it to the Internet themselves by buying a connection to the Internet from an ISP. This was a good way forward at the time, but as the Internet rapidly expanded and became more complex, ISPs themselves started offering hosting services.

Website hosting is now mainly done through ISPs. There are two options:

- renting space on a web server that also has other organisations' websites on it (rather like renting a drawer in a filing cabinet);
- getting the ISP to host your own server, i.e. buying your own computer and having the ISP manage it for you (like buying your own filing cabinet).

Since your website is referenced by your own unique website address (URL), users of your site see only your site and there is no issue with whether you have your own server or share it with others. In reality, this all forms part of the invisible plumbing of the Internet and is of little real concern to web users.

Which option you choose depends on the size and nature of your website. If you are considering getting into e-business in a serious way then the latter option is probably the better as it gives you complete control over the physical machine and security.

There are various benefits to having an expert third party manage your web server for you. These include:

- It is cheaper than doing it yourself with the need for expert staff.
- You do not have to deal with the security issues yourself, which now requires a high level of expertise.
- You do not have to maintain the computer yourself as it becomes somebody else's responsibility to keep it up and running.
- Third parties can offer ongoing support and website development services if you need them.
- ISPs can also register and provide domain name hosting services, which requires increasing expertise as the web becomes more complex.

What is bandwidth?

If you imagine that the usefulness of the Internet depends on the speed at which you are able to bring up web pages, browse them, jump between links and download information onto your own computer, it becomes clear that the size of the link between your machine and your ISP is important. In simple terms it is like the difference between accessing the water mains either by a drinking straw or a full size mains pipe – in some circles a connection to the Internet is called a pipe. Squeezing information down a drinking straw, an ordinary telephone line is obviously going to be much slower than pushing it down a large pipe.

Communications options

There are various communications options for law firms and their connection to the Internet. This area is in flux and new options are emerging all the time. However, the basics are as follows.

Dial-up versus permanent

There are two types of connection – dial-up and permanent. As the names imply, with a dial-up connection you dial up your ISP when you want to download e-mail and surf the Internet. By definition this is slower. A permanent connection is always on and hence you have 24-hour access to e-mail and the Internet. The practical difference is that with a permanent connection e-mail will arrive directly into your inbox whereas with dial-up it will only be downloaded as often as you dial in. However, it is possible to set up your system to dial in on a regular basis, for example every half an hour or twice a day or whatever suits you to access your e-mail.

Bandwidth options

The current options using telephone lines are:

- 28.8 K modem;
- 56 K modem;
- ISDN line;
- ADSL line;
- leased lines of various bandwidths.

There are other options such as cable, wireless and satellite, but telephone lines are the most popular. It is worth investigating whether local TV and telephone cable companies in your area provide data services.

ISDN

Integrated Services Digital Network (ISDN) standards first appeared in the mid-1980s and have been used in the corporate world for several years. The main benefit of ISDN is that it allows the use of ordinary copper telephone wires but enables much greater transmission speeds (up to 14.4 kilobytes per second (kbps) for basic rate ISDN and 1.54 megabytes per second (Mbps) for premium rate ISDN). However, this is now starting to be eclipsed by ADSL.

ADSL

Asymmetric Digital Subscriber Loop (ADSL) technology is also known as broadband. DSL technology was first introduced by Bell Corporation in 1989 as a way of sending video and television signals from the telephone central office to end users over the ordinary copper wire telephone lines. There are many types of DSL technology and ADSL is the most widely available. The 'asymmetric' part refers to the fact that the technology has been designed to allow much faster download than upload, that is the line operates at different speeds away from and towards the user. Large sized files, for example video files, are sent downstream at a fast rate (typically 1.5–6.14 Mbps), whereas information being sent back from the user (upstream) works at a much slower rate (typically 176–640 kbps). Unlike normal telephone connection ADSL allows for a permanent 24-hour connection.

Most serious businesses will be using ISDN, ADSL or leased lines to connect their own network to the Internet, with modems now being the preserve of the home user or very small firms.

The bottom line is that fast is best. To quote, 'You can never be too rich, too thin or have too much bandwidth'!

The main issue at present for law firms is local availability of ADSL. It is not yet universally available and at the time of writing roll-out is still dependent on British Telecom making a commercial judgement about demand.

How do you build a website?

As we have seen, websites are simply pages of information linked together with hyperlinks. They can be as simple or as complex as you like. The first page, called the home page, usually provides a route to the rest of the site.

The basic technology used to build a website is HyperText Markup Language (HTML), but these days a plain HTML site looks rather dated. Instead website developers use a range of software packages to make their sites look very attractive and they can create some amazing effects. While the professionals might code their sites directly in HTML or XML, the software packages available also enable non-programmers to build good looking websites. Table 2.4 lists some of the current most popular software packages.

Table 2.4 Popular software packages and their uses

Software package	Supplier	Used for
Dreamweaver	Macromedia	Developing websites. This is still probably the most popular professional developers' tool
Flash	Macromedia	Animating graphics and web pages
Flashplayer		Free downloadable player that only plays content created via Flash. This is generally lightweight web-based content – design, animations, user interfaces, etc. – suitable for web deployment via browsers
Ultradev	Macromedia	This is used to develop web pages that take information from databases and present it via active server pages (ASPs). This is the most likely tool for e-business applications
Fireworks	Macromedia	Web graphics (creating, editing and animating), both bitmap and vector (i.e. if you resize the window the image also resizes). Also used for optimising/compressing images. Tightly integrated with other Macromedia products (i.e. the default graphics program when using/inserting images in DW/UltraDev, etc.)

Table 2.4 (*continued*)

Software package	Supplier	Used for
Photoshop	Adobe	Editing graphics for web pages
Shockwave	Macromedia	Free downloadable player. Often confused with Flashplayer although a separate technology. Shockwave plays content created by Macromedia Director. Creates far richer multimedia content (3D/CBT/interactive, etc.) – suitable for web deployment on multiple media (CD/DVD/web, etc.)
FrontPage	Microsoft	Developing web pages

What are HTML and XML?

Put simply, HTML is a way of tagging text – rather like the codes that formatted text and that could be seen with 'Reveal Codes' in the old WordPerfect days – so enabling it to be formatted and displayed in a web browser. What HTML also provides is the ability to link one bit of text to another, the hyperlink, which is at the heart of the World Wide Web.

However, in reality this becomes rather limited quite quickly. HTML was designed only as a way of formatting pages of text with hyperlinks in a web browser and, whilst this is very useful and provides the bare bones of any website, more serious applications need something more sophisticated, enabling a more database-oriented approach to creating and managing sites.

XML (eXtended Markup Language) provides the same functionality as HTML, and is an extension of it. It was officially born in December 1997 as a result of a working group funded by the World Wide Web Consortium, and has become the de facto standard for web-based information.

What XML enables is only just beginning to be exploited. Table 2.5 illustrates some of the differences between XML and HTML. The ability to create names or tags (for example, a client name) is very significant because if everyone in an industry – in this case the legal software industry – uses the same names (or tags) for text, the problem of exchanging information between different systems disappears. It is interesting to note that this is

Table 2.5 Differences between HTML and XML

HTML	XML
HTML is used to format the content of text and there is no way to amend the presentation once it is coded	XML cannot only describe the format of the text, but also its presentation, i.e. you can program it and it can change depending on conditions that you set
Usually you can only easily read HTML with a browser (although word processors also allow this)	Text can be read, exchanged and manipulated with many different types of applications (e.g. databases and spreadsheets) as well as word processors and browsers
No security features	Allows for certain sections of text to be edited, with others as 'read only' depending on the access rights of the user (particularly useful for legal documents!)
No data features	Text can be labelled with names and can then be used to write into and out of databases

not limited to describing information for use on the web. In reality, it forms a very useful schema for describing information for more general-purpose databases as well, i.e. those used by practice and case management systems.

This has been recognised by the Legal Software Suppliers Association who are currently working and consulting on a set of XML tags for legal software applications (see their website at **www.legaltechnology.com**). If and when legal software suppliers adopt these standards, then issues about integrating practice management systems with case management systems could become a thing of the past.

Sound and vision on the web

Graphics produced by graphic designers or captured using digital cameras can be readily incorporated into web pages as images. The two standard file formats most commonly used are GIF (Graphics Interchange Format) and JPEG (Joint Photographics Experts Group). GIF files are limited to 256 colours and are best used for small simple graphics such as banner advertisements, whilst JPEG files are best used for larger images such as photographs where image quality is important.

GIFs can also be animated like cartoons and used for inter-active banner adverts; these require a plug-in to run. Plug-ins are additional programs that provide functionality not present in the standard web browser. They are usually available free of charge over the Internet. Plug-ins can be tiresome if you are operating a tight security system as many corporate firewalls (more about firewalls later in the chapter) will not allow the downloading of software from the Internet. Well-known plug-ins include Adobe Acrobat Reader (for displaying and printing .pdf files) and Macromedia's Flash and Shockwave players.

It is also possible to put audio and video files on websites and make these available in real time to users (this is known as streaming). Streaming media are now used on many sites as they enable the content to start playing within a few seconds. Formats for streaming media have been developed by Real Networks and their plug-ins can be downloaded from **www.realnetworks.com**.

Using databases for websites

Originally websites consisted of series of pages like leaves from a book that were linked together with hypertext. These worked well, and many websites are still built in this way using HTML. As the range of functionality needed on websites increases, however, more and more sites are using databases to hold the information and ASPs (active server pages) to present information from the database to the user.

Most e-business sites now have some form of database under-pinning them. When a user comes onto the website it is possible to select specific information of interest to that user from the database and present it to them on the web page.

This is important for a number of reasons:

- Splitting up information in a database and holding it as indi-vidual items means that if one piece of it changes, you need only change that part once in the database. If, however, it is hardwired onto a page of text (as with HTML) then you would need to redo the whole page.
- You can pick and choose items of information depending on who the user is. The normal way to do this is to have the user log on using some form of user ID and password; you can then present information specific to that user ID.
- Databases are designed to search and sort information, and

this means that websites become easier to search and relevant information easier to find.

- You can design active server pages as a series of templates to hold the information from the database. Again this means that you need only change the template once to have the changes reflected across the board.
- It is easier to maintain information in a database than on hardwired pages as the information can be described by means of a field name, e.g. client name.
- It is easier to collect information from a web page. For example, when you want to collect information from the users of the site using a form, the information can be stored directly into the database from the website and is then easily retrievable as data. This can be done in HTML, but involves you in having to manually extract the information from the form.
- The database approach means that organisations can update their own information on the website rather than relying on website designers and technicians. This usually involves the development of a content management system. Most users are now familiar with some form of database package such as an accounts or practice management system, and so this makes the website easier to update and maintain by the people who actually generate the information in the first place.

Java

Java is a programming language designed for web page development. It is often used to build small application modules (applets) that can be downloaded to a web page and which enable the user to interact with the page (for example, by filling in their contact details) and then send this information back to the web server.

CGI

This is something that you will often see web hosting companies listing as one of their selling points – that they have a full 'list of CGI scripts' available for use.

The Common Gateway Interface (CGI) is a standard for communicating between web documents, and a CGI script is a program that uses this standard to dynamically interact with web documents, such as HTML documents, text files or image files.

For example, a search engine such as Lycos uses a CGI script to take the keyword typed in by the user to search its database and return the results to the web browser. There is more about search engines and keywords in Chapter 7.

Security on the Internet

Security is a hot topic on the Internet and something that law firms are very keen to get right. However, security is an issue that is not simply related to the Internet. As one leading legal IT commentator put it some years ago, many firms are still willing to give an envelope of highly sensitive documents to a man in a wet-suit to carry across town (a motor bike courier) whilst remaining very protective about sending e-mail. Internet security is not foolproof, but has become very sophisticated in the past few years, as befits a medium that is increasingly being used as a mainstream distribution channel by large commercial and financial organisations. More in-depth information on the subject of Internet security can be found in *Managing Cyber-Risks* by Rupert Kendrick (Law Society Publishing, 2002).

Principles of secure systems

These fall into four main areas:

- *authentication* – how do you know the information is from the source it seems to be from?
- *authority* – this involves the issue of digital signatures. Has the author legally consented to something?
- *privacy and confidentiality* – is the transaction data protected? The client may want their transaction to be anonymous. Are all the non-essential traces of the transaction removed from the public network, and all intermediary records eliminated?
- *risk management* – this involves protecting information from viruses, worms and other forms of creepy crawlies that inhabit the Net with malevolent intent.

Security has several different aspects which can be summarised as access, data, protocols, information and transactions. Each security system involves some method of keeping information hidden from third parties who should not be able to access the system.

Digital certificates (keys)

Encryption is a method which ensures that unauthorised users cannot read your information. The encryption process encodes the information in such a way that only the sender and the intended recipient can understand it. A mathematical algorithm is used to scramble the information and this can be decoded only by the use of a 'key'.

Digital signatures

A digital signature is not a scanned image of a handwritten signature. Rather, it is an electronic substitute for a handwritten signature and has been designed to perform the same function. Technically speaking, again it is a code that is scrambled and unscrambled by using your key. By adding this to a digital document, it can be easily verified who signed it, when it was sent and whether the document has been altered during transit.

The public key infrastructure (PKI) and certification authorities

In order for digital signatures and public key encryption to be effective, it is important to be sure that the key intended for decryption of the document actually belongs to the person you believe is sending the document. The developing solution to this is the concept of a Trusted Third Party (TTP). The TTP issues a certificate containing owner identification and a copy of the public key of that person. TTPs are usually referred to as certification authorities (CAs). It is likely that banks and post offices will fulfil this role. The Law Society may also be a TTP for e-conveyancing transactions, authenticating solicitors.

The best know commercial certification authority is Verisign (**www.verisign.com**) commonly used for verification by current e-commerce merchants. For example, the Avon site uses Verisign to prove to its customers that it is the genuine site. Post Offices and telecommunications suppliers are also acting as CAs. Examples include BT (Trust Wise) and Post Office (ViaCode).

The Electronic Communications Act 2000 sets out a framework for the use of electronic signatures.

Virtual private networks

A virtual private network (VPN) is a private wide area network that runs over the Internet rather than a more expensive bespoke private network using expensive leased lines. The technique by which VPNs operate is sometimes referred to as tunnelling, and involves encryption using a secure form of the Internet Protocol know as IPSec.

Table 2.6 describes some of the most popular security standards used on the Internet.

Table 2.6 Current approaches to e-business security

Standard	Function	Used By
SSL (Secure Sockets Layer)	Provides security for data packets at the network level	Internet applications (e.g. web browsers, web servers, etc.)
S-HTTP (Secure HTTP)	Provides security at web transaction level (e.g. uploading and downloading web pages)	Internet applications
PGP (Pretty Good Privacy)	Provides encryption for e-mail whilst being transmitted	Secure e-mail transmission for important information
Secure MIME	Provides security for e-mail attachments (i.e. the documents that you attach to e-mails)	Secure e-mail applications with encryption and digital signatures
SET (Secure Electronic Transaction)	Provides security for credit card transactions	Payments and debits over the Internet

Viruses, worms and other creepy crawlies on the Net

There has been much publicity about these and when the word security is mentioned, computer viruses are often the first thing that comes to mind. So what are they and should you be afraid?

What exactly is a virus?

A virus is a piece of programming code, usually in disguise, that causes some unexpected and usually undesirable event. A virus is often designed so that it is spread automatically to other computer users. Viruses can be transmitted as attachments to an e-mail message, as downloads, or be present on a diskette or CD. The source of the e-mail message, downloaded file, or diskette you've received is often unaware of the virus. Some viruses wreak their effect as soon as their code is executed; others lie dormant until circumstances cause their code to be executed by the computer. Some viruses are playful in intent and effect (displaying Happy Birthday, Ludwig! on your computer screen) and some can be harmful, erasing data or causing your hard disk to require reformatting.

www.whatis.com

Generally, there are three main classes of virus:

- *File infectors*. Some file infector viruses attach themselves to program files, usually selected .com or .exe files. Some can infect any program for which execution is requested, including .sys, .ovl, .prg and .mnu files. When the program is loaded, the virus is loaded as well. Other file infector viruses arrive as wholly-contained programs or scripts sent as an attachment to an e-mail.
- *System or boot-record infectors*. These viruses infect executable code found in certain system areas on a disk. They attach to the DOS boot sector on diskettes or the Master Boot Record on hard disks. A typical scenario is to receive a diskette from an innocent source that contains a boot disk virus. When your operating system is running, files on the diskette can be read without triggering the boot disk virus. However, if you leave the diskette in the drive, and then turn the computer off or reload the operating system, the computer will look first in your A drive, find the diskette with its boot disk virus, load it, and make it temporarily impossible to use the hard disk.
- *Macro viruses*. These are among the most common viruses, and they tend to do the least damage. Macro viruses infect your Microsoft Word application and typically insert unwanted words or phrases.

Virus protection

The best protection against a virus is to know the origin of each program or file you load into your computer or open from your e-mail program. Since this is difficult, you can buy anti-virus software that can screen e-mail attachments and also check all of your files periodically and remove any viruses that are found. From time to time, you may get an e-mail message warning of a new virus. Unless the warning is from a source you recognise, chances are good that the warning is a virus hoax.

Virus hoaxes

A virus hoax is a false warning about a computer virus. Typically, the warning arrives in an e-mail message or is distributed through a message in a firm's internal network. These messages are usually forwarded using distribution lists and they will typically suggest that the recipient forward the message to other distribution lists.

If you get a message about a new virus, you can check it out by going to one of the leading websites that keep up with viruses and virus hoaxes (**www.znet.com**). If someone sends you a message about a virus that you learn is a virus hoax, then let the sender know.

What is a worm?

A worm is a self-replicating virus that does not alter files but resides in active memory and duplicates itself. Worms use parts of an operating system that are automatic and usually invisible to the user. It is common for worms to be noticed only when their uncontrolled replication consumes system resources, slowing or halting other tasks.

How do we protect ourselves?

There is no substitute for good security policies and procedures, coupled with rigorously updated anti-virus software and a firewall. It is also necessary to keep your software regularly updated with patches from software vendors, particularly Microsoft. This is because the creators of viruses and other nasties tend to focus their attention on Microsoft products, especially networking products and e-mail such as Outlook. As each new hole in security is discovered, Microsoft releases a security update to cover it. It is vital that you keep on top of these developments, either through in-house or external means.

Risk management: about firewalls

A firewall is a series of components usually comprising both hardware and software used to filter access to and from the outside world over the Internet. They are designed to control unwanted users – or hackers – from getting into your firm's network if it is linked to the Internet. The word firewall is now used to cover a wide range of security issues, but technically refers only to the part that keeps unauthorised users out. However, it is now usual for incoming e-mail and attachments to be scanned automatically for viruses before reaching the firewall and to all intents and purposes it forms part of the same security system.

What's the difference between an intranet, an extranet and the Internet?

One of the key points about the technologies described above is that they can be used inside organisations as well as out on the Internet. What this means is that the Internet tools, for example a web browser and web pages, can be used for internal systems as well as on the Internet.

This is particularly useful for information intensive organisations such as law firms where a great deal of intellectual property is encapsulated in documents. Various knowledge management tools have been around for years, and the larger law firms have been using document management packages to help them organise and disseminate documents. However, web technologies provide a new level of functionality, particularly in the area of free text searching and linking documents together using hyperlinks.

What is an intranet?

An intranet can be described simply as a website which uses all the usual features of websites, but which is only accessible to staff of the firm. The useful information on this internal website could include:

- leave and sickness forms which can be filled in online and routed for authorisation to the person in charge;
- the office manual, with hyperlinked text making navigation more user friendly;
- a firm-wide diary to see who is in and who is out as well as managing key dates and resources such as meeting rooms;
- precedents – legal know-how searchable with free text search;
- templates, documents and forms – easily accessible using hypertext links.

Most firms have this kind of functionality available already using standard Windows features and practice and case management systems. The point of an intranet is that it provides one port of call, saving users the need to navigate around the folder and file structures of their desktop and servers. Using web technologies, functionality such as the ability to fill in forms online and have these routed to the correct person as well as having the information automatically read into a database is now feasible and affordable.

If you would like an overview of what an intranet can do check out **www.intranets.com** (an American intranet application service provider) which has a useful explanation, together with audio commentary.

What is an extranet?

An extranet is a website that is made available to limited classes of people outside the organisation, for example clients, counsel, estate agents and other third parties. Invariably an extranet is used to provide another channel of communication with the outside world, where information is stored that is of interest to those third parties and is made available as a value added service. Law firms are starting to experiment with extranets, making key matter information available to clients on a secure website. There is much more on this topic in Chapter 5.

Some other emerging technologies

New ideas are emerging almost daily. It is impossible to predict what will take off and what will fail, but here are some of the hot topics of the moment.

Portals

The word 'portal' has a range of different meanings to different users. In simple terms it describes a website, internal or external, that collates information on a particular topic or sector. More complex software is emerging to automate some of the functions needed to keep information accessed through the portal up to date. Some portal software aims at recognising individual users and building up a pattern of their information usage so that it can simply present information relevant to their needs. Larger organisations are starting to use portal software to manage the integration of their intranets, extranets and websites.

SMS text messaging

Text messaging is becoming increasingly popular, and many specialist legal case management systems now integrate it into their software. This enables a text message to be sent to clients when a key stage of their matter is reached or when contact needs to be made.

Personal digital assistants

PDAs are essentially very small hand-held computers or mobile phones. Typical functionality includes receiving and sending e-mail and surfing the Internet as well as being able to type or write documents in Word and have calendar, scheduling and contact management similar to Outlook. Some PDAs also incorporate digital camera features with the ability to send picture e-mail.

Some specialist legal software suppliers are incorporating the use of PDAs for off-site time recording and document production. These tools look set to become very popular with practitioners who need to spend a lot of time out of the office, for example at court.

Bluetooth

This technology defines a set of standards for computers, mobile phones and PDAs to interconnect with each other and with home and business telephones using a short-range wireless connection. For example, users of this technology will be able to synchronise information on their PalmPilot with their desktop

PC, or initiate sending and receiving a fax, and in general have all mobile and fixed computer devices totally coordinated.

General packet radio service

GPRS is a mobile phone technology that promises to make it possible and cost effective to remain constantly connected to the Internet via a mobile phone. Much higher data speeds than currently available are also promised and GPRS should become much more widely available in the UK in the near future.

Other wireless technologies

It is becoming increasingly possible to log onto wireless networks to access the Internet in key hot spots, for example mainline railway stations. With the right card installed in your laptop, you can simply connect without the use of a modem or telephone line. Coverage at present is patchy and unreliable, but this could become the way of the future.

3

E-business and law firms

What's possible and what are firms doing?

In the beginning

In October 1994, the Law Society held its annual Solicitors Conference with a session dedicated to legal information technology (IT) sponsored by BT and Microsoft. The session took the form of a short play about two solicitors collaborating on a commercial contract. The play featured live use of video teleconferencing and e-mail and the denouement was the fact that one solicitor was supposedly in the UK and the other in New York. Interestingly the whole play took place without a single mention of the Internet or the World Wide Web. The infrastructure being suggested for use in the play was a mixture of ordinary and leased telephone lines, no easy thing to set up, as some heart-stopping moments behind the scenes proved. Within a few months, by April 1995, the Internet had exploded into popular consciousness and the Law Society was experimenting with its own website.

Defining e-business

As we saw in Chapter 1, the most basic definition of e-business is using the Internet to connect to customers, partners and suppliers.

In the legal world, this translates into connecting with clients, legal agencies, and others in the legal supply chain, e.g. counsel, other lawyers, estate agents, online legal information providers, office stationery suppliers – in essence anyone who provides goods or services which are part of legal business. But the term also implies the transformation of existing business processes to make them more efficient. To be able to engage in e-business successfully, law firms need to be able to unlock their knowledge and client information so they can share this information and conduct transactions with clients and other interested parties via the Internet. For some firms this may involve adopting new web-enabled business models and completely new ways of undertaking core legal business processes.

E-business can improve the way a firm does business by providing a new medium for:

- collecting money from clients and suppliers – the supply chain;
- improving the productivity of current business processes, in particular the distribution of information;
- developing and supporting new automated processes – doing old things differently and doing new things that couldn't be done before without the technology;
- changing how the firm deals with existing and new clients.

The business of law, being essentially an information exchange business, is particularly well suited to e-business and what it has to offer. While it seems that the threat that the Internet would cause a wholesale revolution in the legal industry seems to be fading, an evolution to completely web-enabled legal business is inevitable.

Large organisations such as financial institutions, banks and supermarket chains, have invested heavily in making the Internet work for them. The British government has also announced ambitious plans to enable citizens to interact with government electronically by 2008. Whether this will be achieved is debatable; however, what is not in dispute is the commitment to the idea of the digital society. Lawyers are now aware of the push towards e-conveyancing and these types of initiatives are set to increase as government starts to explore the Internet as a medium for managing governmental processes and costs.

E-business and business pressures on law firms[1]

E-business offers some new opportunities for dealing with some of the business pressures that face law firms. The past decade has seen a major shift in the way legal business operates, with some of the age-old certainties being eroded to the point of extinction. These changes fall into three broad areas:

- client expectations;
- competition;
- technology.

Client expectations

Clients have become consumers, used to shopping around on price, treating professionals as mere service providers, and complaining when the service doesn't meet their standards. Client loyalty can no longer be counted on in a buyers' market. Commercial clients have become even more demanding, expecting transparency and proof of value-for-money – requiring law firms on their panels to go through beauty parades and re-bid for their custom on a regular basis.

Competition

Competition is on the increase, and not just from other law firms. Increasingly, marketing organisations using sophisticated techniques are attracting clients who are then farmed out to solicitors on their panels. Banks and estate agents are setting up their own in-house services or setting up panels of firms. Organisations like Citizens Advice Bureaux are also becoming more proactive in providing their legal services, and insurance companies and trade unions now offer legal advice as part of their policies/services to their members. Increasingly the high street firm is not getting work directly from the client, but having to deal with one or other of these types of intermediary, introducing a new element into their traditional marketing strategy.

These intermediaries are all investing heavily in e-business technologies to deliver some part of their services. For example Legal Marketing Services has its online STARS milestone system to track progress of matters referred to solicitors. A number of specialist legal software suppliers are building interfaces from their practice and case management systems to these bulk referrers.

Ways of competing

The traditional ways of competing in the business world are to pitch the following variables relative to the type of market you are in:

- price of goods/service;
- quality of goods/service;
- distribution – time and place of delivery;
- service – client care, speed of work, relationship management.

Law firms cannot compete in the usual way on price and quality of work and attempts to do this in the past have met with disaster. Many firms offering the £99 conveyance in the early 1990s soon discovered that this was uneconomic. As a regulated professional service there is no opportunity to offer 'poorer quality' legal advice. This leaves the other factors of distribution and service. Law firms seeking to differentiate themselves from the competition can look at these two areas and see what leverage e-business technologies can bring.

Technology

Richard Susskind[2] talks about the impact that the automatic teller machine (ATM) had on the banking industry. The ATM did not replace an existing way of delivering a service (a hand coming out of the wall at midnight clutching cash!), but invented an entirely new way of delivering a needed service.

Technology is providing ever new ways to do things and other areas of business are embracing them. Online services on the Internet, available 24 hours a day, seven days a week, are becoming commonplace, for example, buying books, airline tickets and insurance, and there has been a major increase in the 'Direct' type of services using a combination of telephone and websites, all improving the speed and efficiency of service for consumers. This trend makes companies that are not operating in this way look old-fashioned and out of touch. With FedEx you can now track the delivery of your parcel around the globe, and with Dell request a custom assembly of a computer and then track its progress from the factory to your door using their website. As companies and their consumers grow ever more sophisticated in this way, legal services need to keep up.

Legal business on the web: the story so far

Around a third of law firms in England and Wales have websites. There have also been lots of experiments with online legal services, some of which have been more successful than others.

The initial focus for law firms has been on having a web presence, rather than thinking what the site is actually for. The overall consensus at present is that a website is a marketing tool in the broadest sense of the word. E-business takes this one step further and looks at how to web-enable the whole practice rather than just the marketing processes. The various stages in this development are outlined below.

Many different sorts of website have emerged in the legal market with a range of different functionalities. Although it is difficult to categorise them what follows is an attempt to do so. Marketing sites include:

- brochureware sites;
- content-rich sites;
- online legal services;
  - the document approach;
  - other approaches;
  - virtual legal services.

Marketing websites

> First we thought the PC was a calculator. Then we found out how to turn numbers into letters with ASCII – and we thought it was a typewriter. Then we discovered graphics, and we thought it was a television. With the World Wide Web, we've realized it's a brochure.
>
> Douglas Adams

Brochureware sites

As noted in Chapter 1 around 80 per cent of current law firm websites fall into this category. These sites fall into two distinct camps:

- *The DIY sites*. These were typical of the early days (1995/96) and have a very home grown look and feel. They tended to be built by the likes of computer science students and gifted amateurs with a skill for coding in HTML. Some sites from this era still remain and are now looking very dated. Make sure yours isn't one of them!

- *The corporate identity sites.* These tend to be built by public relations, marketing and design agencies and follow the style of a corporate brochure. They may include animations using Flash (see Chapter 2).

Both types of site are simply online brochures that talk about the firm and outline its services, and may or may not have facilities for people to respond by e-mail. The main intention of these sites is to be seen to have a presence on the Internet. In the early days it was hoped that the site would bring in additional business, but this rarely works unless it has a specific focus and is marketed offline.

Brochureware sites show the firm's personality and clients and would-be employees often use them to appraise a firm. Practical uses also include instructions on how to find the firm. A basic website of this sort is now a necessity for all firms regardless of size.

Content-rich sites

These sites offer content to the user in the form of information that the firm thinks will be of use to visitors. This can vary from legal forms to articles and digests on the law.

The problem with this kind of site is that unless the firm has a dedicated resource to continuously amend, update and grow the information, they rapidly get out of date. There is also the problem of trying to be all things to all people. Unless the site is tightly targeted at a specific type of audience, they can quickly become an untidy listing of unrelated documents which users find hard to navigate.

Online legal services

The main difference between online service sites and content-rich sites is the level of interactivity. By definition online legal services will require some level of input from the user to enable the information to be tailored to their needs.

To find out the latest on what law firms are doing visit **www.venables.co.uk**. This site is useful for keeping track of latest developments where you can undertake your e-business research and keep an eye on the competition. Venables talks about the various approaches that law firms are currently taking in offering online services. The following is a very brief overview.

The document approach

A lot of online legal services adopt the document approach. This makes sense since most legal know-how is captured in documents of one sort or another. The basis of this approach is that a firm will have a set of precedents or templates. How the online client interacts with these varies and there are various flavours of service. These are explained in Table 3.1.

Table 3.1 The document approach

Service	Description
Fact sheets	This is probably the simplest model of online service where legal information is provided in bite-size pieces around specific legal problems, e.g. unfair dismissal or what to do as a driver in a traffic accident. There is a thin line between information and advice here and firms need to be clear exactly what they are offering. Users may be asked some simple questions to filter the correct fact sheets
Document merge	This is very similar to a mail merge in word processing. The client fills in an information form online and information from this form is then merged into the relevant template. The client then prints this out on their own printer. This approach works well for standard types of documents, e.g. wills or filling in predefined forms
Document assembly	This is a rather more sophisticated version of document merging. Here the online client not only fills in key information that will be merged into the document, but also answers key questions about their matter. The document assembly tool then selects appropriate clauses to be assembled into the document and the online client is presented with a document that is more closely allied to their particular concerns. This approach works well for those cases where it is possible to develop standard clauses on an 'if x is true then y clause applies' basis

Table 3.1 (*continued*)

Service	Description
Package of documents	This approach provides a standard set of documents for a particular matter type and the online user applies it to their particular circumstances. There may be document merging and assembly facilities incorporated. The point is to provide the whole range of documents needed for a particular legal process, e.g. divorce
Subscription	With this approach, the online user pays a subscription to the provider of the service and then has access to a library of information they can search and sort according to their specific requirements
Pay-per-view	With this approach the user buys a specific document type on a one-by-one basis. Some services also offer a telephone facility where the online client can ring up and get advice (at premium line rates) on how to use the document

Other types of online service

Other types of online legal services that are not particularly document based are described in Table 3.2. These services are usually incorporated into a website which may be of the corporate brochure style.

Table 3.2 Other types of online service

Service	Description
Calculators	Online facilities to do calculations for such things as: • employment loss • welfare benefits • child support
Corporate legal content provision	One enterprising firm provides legal content for the top 100 FTSE sites. This means that the companies do not have to worry about providing up-to-date legal information to their customers as this is provided by the law firm. It is an extension of the client newsletter approach

Table 3.2 (*continued*)

Service	Description
Tender management	Another organisation run by lawyers provides online tendering management for companies seeking legal services. They are, in effect, project managers for a legal services tender process
Niche sites/portals	These seek to provide a one-stop information solution for tightly focused legal problems, e.g. unfair dismissal, by providing not only information, but also forms and documents and links to other relevant sites. By being tightly focused they become a service in that the user does not have to shop around to find other relevant information – the service is in knowing that everything that is needed is provided in one place
Online quotations	This is probably the most common form of online service very popular for conveyancing. The online client fills in relevant information, e.g. purchase price, and is told what their conveyance will cost. More sophisticated versions will also include all disbursements

Virtual Legal Services

There is also a wave of online legal service providers which seek to operate independently (or seemingly independently) from law firms. These organisations have tried to analyse what legal services actually comprise and offer new types of services in new ways delivered purely online, which is different from offering them as part of a bricks and mortar law firm.

The best known of these is probably Linklaters Blue Flag service. Linklaters has analysed specialist areas of law and developed legal products – documents, commentaries and other ways of delivering know-how – which are available by subscription from their website. They use lawyers to develop and update their products, but the idea is that clients do not have the traditional contact with a lawyer. In theory at least, this means that know-how can be packaged and sold 24 hours a day, seven days a week, which is particularly appealing for international firms with international clients.

Various ways of packaging legal knowledge have been developed by firms and alternative legal service providers, and these usually comprise some kind of document and legal form (see 'The document approach' above). There are around 200 websites offering this type of service – some linked to law firms, some wholly independent. Examples include **www.Freelawyer.co.uk** and **www.Legalshop.co.uk**.

Other virtual working models include using the technology to facilitate groups of lawyers working together as virtual teams on matters (**www.LawGym.com**, **www.V-Lex.com** and **www.FirstLaw.co.uk**). This has the advantage that no premises are required and that lawyers can work from where they choose. The technology enables collaboration between clients and their lawyers with the website as a central 'filing cabinet' which can be accessed via the Internet and a simple web browser.

The web-enabled legal practice

What lies beyond the marketing website is the fully web-enabled legal practice where the Internet and Internet technologies are incorporated in all aspects of the day-to-day working of the firm. This means the firm is making use of Internet technologies to support and enhance its business, as well as using a website to market current and new services. This involves a different mindset from simply having a website, although a site will probably form part of the overall business infrastructure.

Before long the 'e' will probably be dropped from our description of e-business as the Internet and web technologies become deployed in the same way as other technologies, like accounts and time recording software and case management. It is likely that the boundaries between the two will become blurred and possibly disappear altogether as practice and case management software become fully web-enabled. In other words, having a website will disappear as a separate entity and will be regarded as a normal and necessary component of a law firm's business infrastructure, just like a word processing network.

Opportunities for legal e-business

It is very easy to talk about web-enabling legal practices, but what does this mean in reality? The thinking behind serious e-business is to use the technologies and the Internet to support and develop current business processes. Good e-business strategies also make use of the unique features of the Internet and the technologies to be innovative and develop new ways of doing things. But where do you start?

A word about business processes

Describing business in terms of the processes it employs to deliver goods and services to customers and clients has been around a long time. The idea of looking at what people do in their day-to-day tasks, analysing it, and looking for efficiency improvements has been with us since Fredrick W Taylor wrote *The Principles of Scientific Management* in 1911. His ideas are revered in Japan where his concept of scientific management has been used in the development of quality assurance processes that are credited with the Japanese post-war recovery.

In the legal world business processes are probably more familiarly known as practice and procedure. Good examples of business processes are the new procedures set down for Civil Justice – fast tracking cases provides an example of an attempt to re-engineer some age-old practice and procedure in civil litigation.

A starting point: the client and stakeholders

A very good starting point when thinking of developing e-business capability is to look at the business processes that impact on the client, as they are ultimately the source of income. It may be that the client is not just the individual or organisation for whom you are providing the legal service. In the increasingly complex legal services industry, there may be other players who are stakeholders in what you do and who also need care and attention. Examples are bulk referrers of work and the Legal Services Commission.

Key areas for e-business

In the whole maze of what's possible with e-business, it can be helpful to look at the two main areas that other industries and sectors are using to anchor their e-business propositions. These are:

- client relationship management (CRM);
- supply chain management (SCM).

While providing client care and management is fairly obvious for a law firm, supply chain management is probably less obvious. These two areas are discussed in detail below.

Client relationship management

In an increasingly competitive world, in which consumerism is rife and clients can no longer be taken for granted, a more structured approach is required to gain clients and manage them effectively as the fundamental source of business. The transition from 'profession' to a 'legal services industry' puts the focus on the client. While any worthwhile marketing plan will also focus on the client, marketing as a discipline is more about identifying markets, segmenting them and then developing or tailoring services to meet the needs of that market. In CRM the emphasis is on existing clients so as to deliver better service and more importantly ongoing service to the client. One of the key tenets of CRM is to ensure client loyalty over time.

A methodology for looking at the way you do things is described in the next chapter, meanwhile we shall take a look at the range of things that are possible and that some law firms are already incorporating into their e-business operations.

Client facing business processes

See Table 3.3.

Client extranets

The mechanism used by most law firms to deliver enhanced client care or client relationship management is a client

Table 3.3 Client facing business processes

Business process	Example tasks
Marketing	Attracting clients, either via traditional methods (advertising, word of mouth) or referral agencies, claims farms
Selling	Providing quotations, initial free legal advice sessions
Qualifying the client	Initial check to ensure it's the sort of legal problem you want to deal with, for example no win no fee assessment
Taking instructions	Initial interview, getting admin details, assessment of legal problem and costs, risk assessment
Funding	Advising on costs, getting up-front payments for disbursements, etc., filling in LSC forms
Client care process	Client care letter, terms and conditions sent to client
Doing the legal work	There are ongoing requirements to be in communication with the client. How this works in practice depends very much on the nature of the matter. Interim billing
Client relationship building	This takes place as part of or as an allied activity to the legal work, e.g. providing general information related to the matter, cross-selling, inviting clients to seminars, sending them newsletters
Closing the matter	Final bill, archiving documents, sending relevant documents to client

extranet. In simple terms, this is usually a secure area on a firm's website that clients, or other interested parties, gain access to through using a login ID and a password. Once they have logged in, clients are presented with the information that is relevant to their own particular concerns, i.e. they see only their own information.

Exactly what information the client sees and when is entirely at the discretion of the firm and this is the area where a lot of thought has to be put in as to what will add value to the client.

Matter reporting (status tracking)

Client extranets are becoming very popular for more transaction based types of legal work, such as domestic conveyancing, debt collection and personal injury. In these areas it is possible to develop a milestone approach where key tasks can be identified, for example, exchange of contracts. A list of these milestones is presented to the client with the ones that have been completed ticked off. This kind of 'to do' list approach is probably the simplest to implement and can provide useful tracking information to clients.

The real issue with this type of approach to giving client information is that it tends to provoke more questions than it answers. Many firms implement a client extranet in the hope that it will reduce client telephone calls; unfortunately the opposite tends to be the case as clients, who do not fully understand legal process, will call the law firm to get an explanation of what the milestone means and how important it is.

As a way of dealing with this, it is quite common to annotate the milestones with help text to explain to the lay user what each milestone means and its significance to the overall process. These explanations can be helpful, but need to be kept very brief and as a consequence are very hard to write and get right.

Another issue with the milestone approach is that it reports on what is past, i.e. what has been completed. In reality clients tend to be more interested in the future and what happens next. With this in mind, some firms try to estimate the target completion date for subsequent milestones based on previous ones. This approach has both pros and cons. On the positive side it can help a client get a feel for how the matter has progressed and will progress in the future. On the downside a firm may end up being a hostage to fortune if predicted timescales don't work out according to plan.

A balanced approach needs to be taken to matter progress reporting and very much depends on the clients and the matter type.

Financial reporting

This offers the client the opportunity to see the amount of time recorded and billed together with the amount of outstanding work in progress, the charge-out rates and other financial information that might be useful, e.g. disbursements.

Most firms consider this type of reporting to clients as dangerous territory because bills are often adjusted for a whole range of issues. While for some areas of law this type of reporting will not really add much value to the client, in other areas – particularly those that are less transactional based, for example commercial work and litigation – firms that are able to offer this level of transparency will probably be favoured in the long run.

Online archives

Online archives can be held of all the documents, e-mails and other material related to a matter. As these are held in digital form they can be searched, sorted and catalogued far more easily than the paper version. This also provides an online backup for key materials should there be a problem with the internal systems of a firm.

Virtual deal rooms

This is a piece of jargon that simply describes the ability to store information (e.g. documents, e-mails, and other material) relevant to a particular matter, with a view to making it available to a range of interested parties to the matter, including the client. There is usually the facility to catalogue documents and search, sort and annotate them, as opposed to editing them. The actual use of virtual deal rooms is hard to assess and the general feeling is that those developed by law firms are decreasing in popularity with large corporate clients.

Online project room

This type of facility often overlaps with the virtual deal room and is probably most appropriate for complex litigation where a project management approach enables the effective management of the work. Some form of project planning tool is used to plan key tasks, map them onto charts and allocate work to various resources including fee earners. The purpose of this approach is to ensure that not only time but other resources are managed and that critical areas that affect the progress of the whole are identified and dealt with.

The online aspect of this allows a much higher level of ongoing collaboration than was previously possible, again on a 24 hours a day, seven days a week basis. This can become particularly useful if working across time zones.

Online case management

This is being talked about more and more in the legal market, with some specialist software providers already making their specialist case management available online. In essence what this means is that the firm operates their case management on an external website linked by telephone lines.

If the case management system is hosted on an external website with the appropriate security, remote working, i.e. fee earners working from home or court, becomes feasible since all that is required is a method of accessing the Internet and a web browser. In terms of enabling client extranets, it is then possible to give the client access to limited areas for them to see what is happening on their own matter. In reality this is likely to be summary reports rather than the raw data of day-to-day operations.

This type of service is already available as an application service provision (ASP) service. However, most firms are currently approaching it as a way to cut down internal IT overhead costs and manage their infrastructure more appropriately, rather than seeing it as the first plank in an overall e-business strategy to facilitate client access and transparency.

E-commerce functionality

E-commerce, although sometimes used as an interchangeable term with e-business as we saw in Chapter 1, is about buying and selling on the Internet and the associated transaction processing, such as taking payments over the Internet. This immediately brings up the question of security in most people's minds.

Electronic funds transfer (EFT) is at the heart of e-commerce. Shopping sites on the Internet are alive and well despite the dot.com crash, with, for example, Amazon and Dell proving the value of online shopping.

There are now secure ways of providing credit card information over the Internet. To accept credit cards as a payment option you become a credit card merchant with your bank or credit card organisation. You are then required to pay a percentage fee from

1 per cent to 3 per cent depending on your turnover and the products sold. There are also a number of companies on the Internet who will process credit card information for you once it has been entered into their website.

Credit card processing

After a user has provided you with their credit card details, two things must happen in order to complete the transaction:

1. The credit card must be authenticated with the credit card company so that you can receive an authorisation number. This provides a limited guarantee that the funds will be made available by ensuring the user of the card is not over their limit and the card has not been stolen.
2. The electronic card information must be turned into an actual deposit at your bank.

Some companies (e.g. Cybercash) provide Internet processing software that can accept and process credit card information to receive online authorisations. They can also provide software for linking with your bank to create credit card deposits.

Online banking

Most banks now provide online banking services which many law firms are making use of. Typical functionality includes the ability to:

*   check account balances;
*   transfer funds between accounts;
*   pay bills electronically;
*   apply for loans;
*   download information about accounts;
*   trade shares;
*   view images of cheques and deposits.

There are two ways of doing online banking. The first is to install special software provided by your bank which then dials up the bank's own server. This is called a point-to-point connection. The second way is to access banking services via a website using what is essentially the bank's version of a client extranet. To access it you only need to be able to access the Internet and no special software is required.

For some legal business processes, e.g. conveyancing, EFT is of critical importance. Integrating electronic banking into the overall process therefore makes a lot of sense.

The next major development in online banking will be bill presentment. What this is in essence is presenting the customer/client with an online bill which they then review and authorise for online payment at the click of a button. The client is either alerted by e-mail that there is a bill to review and they then log on to a website to view and pay the bill, or they receive the bill as an e-mail and then log on to a website to authorise payment. The funds are then automatically transferred from their account. This process is different from paying bills electronically which really only deals with part of the billing process. Again this is an example of looking at a whole business process and seeing if delivering it online can add value. Clearly billing is a key concern for law firms and this option may be worth looking at.

E-conveyancing

Progress is being made on e-conveyancing (see **www.egi.co.uk** and **www.landregistry.gov.uk/econveyancing** for more details) and a new framework has received Royal Assent. However, it is likely that it will take until 2005 before pure e-conveyancing becomes normal practice.

In web-enabling the business processes associated with conveyancing some of the key issues associated with all e-businesses are being tackled. These include authentication with the use of digital signatures, as well as making land and local searches available online.

To take advantage of the new electronic environment, conveyancers will need desktop access to the Internet and e-mail, preferably using a broadband link. They will also need to have some form of electronic client/matter management system, if not a full conveyancing case management system and a means of transmitting and receiving information, preferably at the click of a button rather than having to retype information into forms on third party websites. Specialist legal software suppliers are also working on compatibility issues ensuring that their software will be able to send and collect data from the Land Registry and others who play a key role in the conveyancing process. There will also be software involved with setting up correct authentication and encryption systems to ensure data security.

Exactly how this will all work in practice has yet to be finally determined. What is available right now is electronic access to the Land Registry with three companies holding the licence to deliver this service as well as the ability to do some local authority searches electronically. It was recently reported that Countrywide Property Lawyers completed a residential property search in Northampton in only 13 minutes as opposed to the usual 10–25 days taken for the traditional paper-based local authority search using one of the National Land Information Service (NLIS) providers.

The real benefits will come when all the systems both in the law firm and in the external information providers and the Land Registry are seamlessly integrated together with electronic banking. Overall this is likely to take years rather than months to achieve.

Legal agencies

It is not just law firms that are starting to see the benefits from operating their business online. The legal agencies are also experimenting in a serious way with what's possible. New developments are emerging all the time. The following are offered as a brief indicator of the range of e-business activities undertaken by some legal agencies. Check out their websites on a regular basis.

Legal Services Commission

The LSC continues to look at the Internet and how it can be used and has developed a specific e-business area on its website which can be found at **www.legalservices.gov.uk/ebusiness/index.htm**.

The Court Service

The Court Service has started a series of innovative e-business style services, the most recent being 'Money claim online'. The service enables people to make small claims online.

Another service being offered directly to the public is XHIBIT:

> Making court hearings as speedy and effective as possible, to give a real benefit to victims, witnesses and all involved. XHIBIT provides information to the public via screens around the court building and via the Internet.

The parties involved in the cases can receive information via:

- e-mail;
- fax;
- text message (SMS);
- pager.

There is also a range of information and forms available to the public.

Companies House

Companies House now has a web-filing service available. This provides a secure system for presenters to submit company information via the Companies House website. The following document details can now be presented online:

- change of situation or address of registered office;
- appointment of Director or Secretary;
- terminating appointment as Director or Secretary;
- change of particulars for Director or Secretary.

Conclusions

Some overall conclusions can be drawn from what has happened so far in the online legal marketplace:

- As in the wider e-business world, what enjoys most success is the business-to-business (B2B) arena. In the legal world this translates into working primarily with commercial clients who have the Internet at their fingertips and are becoming used to using it for all manner of business, including procuring and using legal services.

- Business-to-consumer/law firm to new client (B2C) activities have had less success. It is difficult to attract new business from legal services websites designed for new clients. Some firms who have implemented third party document assembly solutions in the hope of generating fresh business from their websites have been disappointed.

- A key growth area is working with existing clients and using the Internet to add value as a separate distribution medium, particularly through the use of client extranets. The idea of online legal services is shifting away from trying to attract new business to serving current clients better and more effectively.

- Legal agencies are exploring e-business strategies and can see the potential of huge savings by facilitating the filing of documents, forms and searches online. E-conveyancing is one example, electronically filing Companies House forms is another.

- The next objective is to integrate the Internet into day-to-day operations, eliminating the need for a separate e-business strategy, in others words having the Internet part of the mainstream for key business processes. A simple example of this is the now predominant use of e-mail to send messages and deliver documents.

- The concept of collaboration is coming to the fore, as it is possible to create electronic environments to share know-how, documents, notes, project plans and diaries on a secure website. This creates a working space for all parties involved in a case, from clients, to counsel, to experts.

Notes

1   Adapted from Christian, C. (2002) *Online Strategies for Smaller Law Firms*, **www.legaltechnology.com**.
2   Susskind, R. (1996) *The Future of Law*, OUP.

4

Developing an e-business strategy and design

Here is Edward Bear, coming downstairs now, bump, bump, bump on the back of the head behind Christopher Robin. It is, as far as he knows, the only way of coming downstairs, but sometimes he feels that there really is another way, if only he could stop bumping for a moment and think of it.

A.A. Milne, *Winnie-the-Pooh*

Asking busy fee earners to take time out to consider developing a strategy is rather like Edward Bear's predicament – finding time to stop and do it seems like a good idea but when? However, this doesn't need to be a large and time-consuming exercise, but it is essential if tangible benefits are to be achieved.

This chapter covers what an e-business strategy is and how you should go about developing one. It also discusses how to design your e-business capability by analysing your business processes.

E-business strategy

So how do you start to integrate the Internet into your business? The starting point is to map out an e-business strategy. In reality, e-business does not exist. What is really being looked at is incorporating the Internet, or more accurately e-mail and the World Wide Web, as another distribution channel into your mainstream business. It can also be more than this, since the nature of the Internet allows you to innovate the way you do business to the extent that entirely new processes can be invented.

In formulating a strategy you will need to consider some big questions. What is legal business? What are the most important elements: the nature of the legal advice you provide or the way you provide it? Can you separate the two? What do clients think? Innovation comes from stepping back from the usual way of doing things and imagining the unthinkable. What would be the ideal way to deliver a legal service for both clients and lawyers in the twenty-first century?

Since the primary medium for e-business is the Internet, the temptation is to collapse the idea of an e-business strategy with the technology needed to deliver it. The business part of the strategy disappears as it becomes a plan to purchase IT equipment and software. It is very important, therefore, to keep the strategy service driven rather than technology driven. Focusing on business objectives rather than technology objectives is the key to developing a successful e-business.

The e-business strategy process

There are almost as many approaches to 'doing' strategy as there are business books and gurus. A traditional approach is:

1. Define objectives.
2. Analyse the external and internal environment, using some form of SWOT (strengths, weaknesses, opportunities and threats) analysis.
3. Identify gaps.
4. Develop strategy.
5. Implement.

Put more simply this boils down to:

- Where do we want to be?
- Where are we now?
- What is the gap?
- How do we bridge the gap?

Presented below is a more detailed approach to developing an e-business strategy that is designed to get you thinking and ending up with some practical ideas of how you can engage with e-business in your firm.

Why do we need to think about e-business?

It is highly likely that in your firm you have a range of attitudes towards IT and e-business. It is probable that the concepts and ideas of e-business haven't reached the radar screen of most of your colleagues. This is reflected in the responses to market research conducted by the Law Society (see Chapter 1). Being clear in your own mind and explaining the concept to your colleagues is a very necessary first step. It is essential to get buy-in from your firm and to recognise that this might take some time.

The best focus for e-business is on the client. The technology and business structure follow on from and are defined by your vision of the value you intend to provide to your clients. E-business also provides opportunities to streamline and make cost savings in the supply chain (see 'E-procurement' below), but the key starting point should be your clients.

Here are some reasons for thinking about developing an e-business strategy:

Positive
Expanding your practice
Improving your marketing
Delivering excellent client care
Increasing your competitiveness
Desire to take a leadership position
Innovating service delivery
Cutting time/costs
Client demand
Referrer demand

Negative
Pressure from competition – and not just law firms
Pressure from third parties: bulk referrers, estate agents
Decreasing market share
Worry and concern

Development of any strategy requires time, energy and thought. When the pressure of fee earning is on, action is often tactical rather than strategic. This can result in a piecemeal approach, which when it comes to implementing e-business and its supporting technologies can result in islands or pockets of systems that don't talk to each other. Integration is a key issue, but not just at the technological level. Since we are now talking about something that goes beyond a brochureware website, careful thought is required to set out the new territory on which the firm wants to play.

Finding where to go first has some fairly simple principles. These are:

1. Look for the most important reasons – both positive and negative – as to why you should develop a strategy.
2. Will the partnership support an e-business strategy to deal with some of the leading issues that are facing you today?
3. Start with key drivers:

    (a) What must the firm keep doing well to survive?
    (b) What must the firm do better to stay competitive?
    (c) What are the unspoken fears about the future of the firm?
    (d) What are the possibilities available to the firm?

Table 4.1 presents some broad opportunities and threats. It is a good idea to look at each in turn and think about how it applies to your situation with your specific business and clients.

Table 4.1 Recognising opportunities and threats in e-business

Opportunities	Threats
Building a closer relationship with clients	Losing clients to new (non-legal) entrants offering faster and cheaper legal services online
Cutting costs caused by inefficient supply, service and billing	Finding that the market for legal services in some sectors disappears completely (e.g conveyancing) as it is swallowed up by online mega-providers offering the whole chain of services (e.g. from property supply – estate agents – through surveying and conveyancing to house moving services)
Receiving direct client feedback and communication	Finding internal inertia or politics prevent you from picking up on what clients are saying and making necessary changes. Adhering to the 'we are the professionals, we know best' approach
Recognising a new market niche out of changing client demands	Making wrong decisions about new technology and increasing costs
Reacting faster and being more responsive than competitors	Being paralysed by an inability to understand changes and fear of making wrong decisions

Not surprisingly, many firms have developed their strategies because of concern about their market position, i.e. 'other firms are doing it and so should we'.

Appetite for change

> Never try and teach a pig to sing. It doesn't work and it annoys the pig.[1]

Having completed a thorough review of the territory and maybe gleaned a few ideas along the way it becomes very important to understand your firm's appetite for change. This is possibly the major influence in the development of your strategy and is really the surest indicator as to whether you will succeed with your plans in the long run. Most firms will have a variable appetite for change ranging from very keen to 'leave us alone'. Determining where your firm fits into the pattern also determines how fast and dramatically you can act.

Law firms have had a fairly rough ride in recent years with the amount of change that has been forced upon them by external pressures. This makes being clear about the business benefits of adopting an e-business strategy even more important. What is vital, however, is that this does not get put in the 'too hard' basket. Understanding the appetite for change can allow you to at least pitch your first e-business project at the right level.

E-business has a lot in common with other high-impact strategies. Too little change might have virtually no impact on the final outcome, whereas too much might threaten the fundamentals of the business. It is advisable to implement change incrementally, determining the risk factors, and acceptable levels of risk from the outset.

Finding e-business opportunities

Where do you start to find the e-business opportunities that are going to make a difference to your firm and in particular its bottom line? Current thinking defines two aspects to where e-business can bring advantage: the 'sell' side and the 'buy' side. See Figure 4.1.

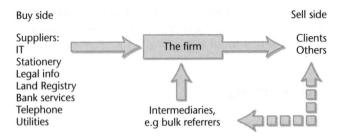

Figure 4.1 Where e-business can bring advantage to your firm

The basic idea is to use the Internet to integrate the inter-actions and transactions your firm has on both sides of the equation. It is perhaps easier to start with the buy side, or e-procurement.

E-procurement

Procurement is the purchasing of product components, standard raw materials, customised supplies, and other goods and services needed to operate a business. In the legal firm context this can range from paper clips to large tenders for IT equipment. The process includes:

- selecting the suppliers;
- submitting formal requests for goods and services to suppliers;
- getting approval from the buyer;
- processing the purchase order;
- fulfilling the order;
- delivery;
- receipt;
- payment.

Starting points for legal e-procurement

It is likely that you are still buying most of your products and services in the traditional paper-based manner. However, you might like to think about starting to use the Internet for making more cost effective purchasing decisions. The first phase of e-procurement is to use the Internet to compare costs across a range of suppliers. For example, you are probably familiar with searching for cheap air flight deals or car hire or hotel rooms using the Internet. Much the same is possible across a wide range of products and services that most law firms use. As a starting point you should consider some of the most commonly used products and services:

- stationery;
- books;
- online legal information (e.g. legal news updates, cases and materials, etc.);
- office furniture;
- IT consumables (e.g. print cartridges);
- payroll services;
- legal forms;
- travel;
- cars;
- utilities;
- communications and telephones;
- cost drafting;
- cleaning;
- DX;
- parcel delivery;
- overflow secretarial services;
- recruitment;
- banking and other financial services;
- magazines and journals.

You can compare prices, delivery times and terms and conditions online across a range of potential suppliers (including your current ones). This is a fast-growing area and more and more suppliers of these types of services are moving towards online ordering. Many suppliers are now also moving towards online billing and payment methods. Using the Internet can allow you to devise a systematic way of purchasing your requirements.

CASE STUDY **Clifford Chance tendering deal with BarclaysB2B, 2 May 2002**

BarclaysB2B, the business-to-business arm of Barclays, today announced it had signed up international law firm Clifford Chance as a major customer to its electronic tender service.

The deal, which initially consists of 15 individual electronic tenders, will help Clifford Chance to manage the purchasing process and costs associated with procurement of capital items, such as office furniture and computer equipment, required for their move to a new London office at Canary Wharf.

BarclaysB2B will provide the training and technical support associated with the electronic tender process, as well as specialist procurement consultancy. Clifford Chance expects to benefit from significant savings on their purchases, and an open and auditable process.

Alison Hutchinson CEO, BarclaysB2B says: 'I am delighted that Clifford Chance have signed up to use our procurement expertise over the coming year. This package of electronic tenders will enable Clifford Chance to manage their supplier relationships more efficiently than ever before.

'With the current challenges of the economy, both the finance and procurement teams at Clifford Chance will be able to directly benefit from the tangible bottom line benefits and management information which our innovation in supply chain management has made possible', she added.

Amanda Burton, Regional Chief Operating Officer for Clifford Chance in London, says 'We are looking forward to our partnership with BarclaysB2B, to using this method of tendering and the potential savings we should make'.

www.newsroom.barclays.co.uk/news/data/708.html

The 'sell' side

Defining client groups

The more complex side of your e-business will relate to your client-facing business.

Start with your client base and define it into groups. This may well be the same process that you have undertaken in developing your marketing plan, as it is essential to segment your market into the types of client groups you wish to serve.

In developing opportunities for e-business, it is important to bring a fresh eye to your client groups. It is very easy to define groups of clients around matter types, e.g. conveyancing clients, personal injury clients, probate clients and so on. Think about grouping your clients according to other factors and see if this brings any fresh insights. Examples could include:

- demographics – age, gender, net worth;
- stage in life – single, just married, with children, retired, new job, just made redundant;
- value to the firm – top clients in terms of fees generated;
- industry sector – for commercial clients;
- techno-competency – don't jump to conclusions here. Assumptions that people over 65 don't use computers is fast becoming a myth;
- interests – depending on the type of work you do, you may well have clients that can be grouped by interest, e.g. golf, football, music business;
- information need – some clients may need far more information than others for whatever reason;
- complexity of matters – grouping clients according to how long and complex their matters are likely to be.

Identifying the needs and desires of each group

This may require that you undertake some research among your clients, formal or informal, to find out what would make a difference to them. Clearly you will need to focus on the issue of the legal services you are delivering, but don't forget other things that may be of interest. For example, if you specialise in employment work, and do a lot of unfair dismissal work, avenues to be explored could also include what sort of support your clients would like around issues of finding new employment, financial planning, etc. Try to get a more holistic picture of what interests your client as this could provide a rich seam to mine when it comes to providing information that adds value to your clients. It may also provide opportunities for referrals to and from other organisations which can be conducted far more easily online.

Defining the best process to deliver value

Having defined what will make a difference to the client group(s) you are focusing on, now take a look at what will deliver value to your client.

There are various ways of doing this and the following are offered as a toolkit to get you thinking. There is no right way to design an e-business. In gaining competitive advantage through providing superior client care it is necessary to be creative and focus on what will make a difference to *your* clients. If you deliver what everyone else is doing you will gain little competitive edge.

Your guiding themes should be:

- to define value elements;
- to integrate all parts of the operation;
- to define value in terms of the whole client experience.

Defining value elements

Look to see where the following factors can be improved:

- *speed* – the rate at which things get delivered to the client;
- *convenience* – clients value one-stop shopping, and integration between online and offline services;
- *personalisation* – clients like to be treated as individuals. Obviously legal advice by its very nature is personal. However, consider that there are extras that you can provide beyond the basic legal advice (e.g., e-newsletters and updates) that can be customised to meet the particular concerns of clients (e.g., in an specific industry sector);
- *price/cost* – value for money is always a key consideration, although remember that your clients may not necessarily be looking for the cheapest.

Integrating business processes

Also look for areas that are currently carried out as separate processes, which the technology now enables you to integrate into a streamlined process. Effective e-business design requires you to identify all the processes with which the client comes into contact and to use technology to integrate these for the client's benefit. Again, think beyond the boundaries of the firm. For example, during a conveyancing transaction, with the client's permission, it may add value to include the estate agent if you decide to update the client by e-mail or SMS text message. Similarly it may be useful to include an accountant or independent financial advisor in relevant aspects of your client's matter. The intention is to create joined up matter handling for the benefit of your clients.

Defining value in terms of the whole client experience: the value network

Think about the context in which your clients are buying your services and see if you can add value. Think through what your client experiences when they interact with your firm and the other organisations involved. A useful way to consider this is to separate the means (services) from the ends (client needs), disassemble the old structure and rethink core capabilities to identify new forms of value.

Look at your client in the widest context and see what comprises value for them across the whole transaction. For example, in the client's mind they are not simply purchasing 'conveyancing'. This is part of a much bigger value chain called 'moving home'. From the client's point of view, estate agents, valuers, mortgage lenders and house removal companies are all part of their experience. In thinking this through, there are a myriad of opportunities, given what the technology makes available, to provide significant added value to clients.

Consider what happens when a client first contacts your firm. It is highly likely that whoever answers the query will first classify the client into a matter type, e.g. conveyancing, personal injury or family. There is nothing wrong with this since most of what solicitors do for their clients is to act as the interface between the client and the legal system they need to go through to get the result they are after. The flavour of the legal system is already predetermined by established procedure and practice in that particular area.

For example, in getting a divorce, a client with children will experience different aspects of the court system, whose own practice and procedure is also organised around procedure types – the divorce procedure, the financial support procedures, the custody procedures – none of which have been designed holistically with the client in mind. It could be argued that this leaves solicitors little room for manoeuvre in terms of creating a different approach based on the whole client experience. Having said this however, there is a vast area of possibility that has yet to be explored by law firms, particularly in relation to developing partnerships with other service and product providers, in the name of providing clients with a better and more integrated experience.

One of the most exciting possibilities made available by the technology is the idea that boundaries between organisations are becoming blurred in pursuit of providing genuine value to customers and clients. At its most simple this can be described as the one-stop shop approach with the intention of providing a client with access to all the services they need for a particular life or business event in one place. This is a different way of looking at who clients are. It is in this area that there will be some true innovation that adds serious value for clients.

It is also the area where the traditional boundaries between law firms and other product and service providers will be eroded. This is the arena of multi-disciplinary practice and the one where the serious competition for law firms will emerge. Law firms that don't think through value from the point of view of their clients will find themselves becoming third party providers to those who take control of the client relationship. To a certain extent this is already happening with the marketing companies that set up closed panels of firms for personal injury and other work. There is an opportunity here for savvy law firms to use e-business opportunities to retake control of the client relationship online. And as all good marketers know, it's the client relationship that counts in generating long-term business.

CASE STUDY | **Creating a value network – linking solicitors, independent financial advisors and accountants**

Organisations other than law firms are beginning to identify the opportunity for building a value network where law firms are one part of a set of services designed to provide a more holistic approach for clients.

A good example of this is ClientMonitor.com which has put together a work referral system among three sets of professionals: independent financial advisors, solicitors and accountants. The basic premise is that each group of professional advisors undertakes a specific business process for their clients, with all potentially having something to offer to the same client. See Figure 4.2.

Figure 4.2 Creating a value network

The idea of referring work between professional service providers is not new and many firms are already doing this with varying degrees of success. However, an e-business approach to this opens up new possibilities that only become available at a reasonable cost when the Internet and a website can be used to provide the infrastructure not only for referring the work, but also for monitoring client progress to predefined quality standards. This offers the comfort that referred clients are being professionally dealt with and that progress can be checked at any time. It also makes managing referral fees and commissions within the various rules set out by the professional bodies more transparent.

Doing this via a secure extranet makes the process cost effective, and while it is still possible to do this without the Internet, using a website as the communications mechanism and the infrastructure for managing the work makes it not only feasible, but easy. The website creates additional support for business processes that are already in place enabling new and better ways of managing them for the benefit of clients.

For more information see **www.clientmonitor.com**.

New business models

A business model is basically a set of processes which provide value (product or service or a mix of both) to clients such that they are prepared to pay money for it. Thinking through an e-business strategy offers you opportunities to go beyond the normal idea of what a law firm is and does and to think about adopting new business models, particularly if you are considering working more closely with third parties external to the firm.

Past business models were developed in a world where people and organisations communicated in a fixed way with fixed roles within fixed organisational boundaries. So, for example, the traditional business model for law firms is that fee earners have one-to-one relationships with clients who are charged for the fee earner's time. The boundary between a law firm and others is fixed, with clients thinking that they know the optimum point to approach a solicitor. Unfortunately, as has often been pointed out, in commercial matters this can often be too late for the lawyer to have a real impact. Commercial lawyers describe working with clients in terms of being the fence at the top of the cliff rather than the ambulance at the bottom. In thinking through the client value chain a new real opportunity exists to become that legal fence.

Another example of an emerging business model is outlined by Susskind[2] who discusses how the legal paradigm may be shifting from one-to-one to one-to-many, with lawyers providing packaged information that is consumed by large numbers online.

E-business relies on the development of new strategies based on the idea of the networked world. It helps to start thinking outside the box about how legal business looks and could look from the client's point of view. The suggestion is not that you radically change the way you work right now, more that you start considering evolving new thinking and ways of working that complement your traditional business model.

Table 4.2 describes some different types of online value propositions.

Table 4.2 Different types of online value propositions

Business model	Value proposition for the client	Example
Infomediary	Provides a one-stop shop for all the information required in a specific area by a client (including their matters). Offers ease of use, quick results and therefore cost savings	Blueflag from Linklaters; Delia Venables portal; client extranets
Transaction intermediary	Provides a unified process for finding, comparing, selecting and purchasing products or services online. Offers speed and cost savings	The online tendering service, Law Management Section
Category leader	Becomes a market leader by identifying a new value proposition and constantly innovating the client experience. Offers the best total customer experience	Blueflag from Linklaters
Community centre	Creates a topic-specific meeting place online where members can interact to share ideas and information. Offers ease of contact and community membership	**www.lawzone.co.uk**
Industry portal	Provides a single, easy-to-use facility for organisations within a specific industry or sector to conduct business-to-business trading. Offers time and cost savings and access to new suppliers	**www.terratorium.co.uk**

Designing the e-business infrastructure

By the time you have developed an e-business strategy which has a broad outline of what you are doing and why, you may have agreed some ideas with external stakeholders, for example a local estate agency or bulk referrer. You should also have discussed ideas with your firm, ideally not just partners, but other fee earners and support staff as well as external advisors like your accountant – all the stakeholders who are likely to be impacted by the plan or who may have a professional interest in it.

This section will help you think through a preliminary design for your e-business, in particular the range and scope of what you intend to do, and discusses a simple technique for analysing business processes.

The elements of e-business design

There are three elements to any e-business design:

- *Business processes*. A business process can be defined as 'who does what when'. The whole point of e-business is that relevant processes are web-enabled providing significant added value for clients and the firm, and that whole new processes are invented that would not be possible in the offline world.
- *The IT infrastructure*. You need to deliver this online and include the use of websites – as an intranet, extranet, public website or some mixture of these – the plumbing for what you want to do.
- *The infostructure*. You have to define the information (content) you want to deliver and where it comes from. Just as you install plumbing to get water to the places it is needed so content can be likened to the water in the pipes. It needs to keep flowing, flow freely and be fresh.

Business process analysis

Examining the existing structure and identifying changes

This is the starting point for turning good ideas into action. If you have been through the strategy process you will have identified some key areas of your practice where you think incorporating the Internet and Internet technologies will make a real difference. As has been emphasised throughout this book, this means a real difference to clients, either directly or indirectly. It is now time to take a closer look at the way you currently work and think through how integrating the Internet might really help in practice.

What is a business process?

At the simplest level, a business process is a set of tasks that you perform in a given order to achieve a predefined outcome. A simple low level example is 'Produce document'. This business process may comprise a variety of tasks depending on the way you like to work.

'Produce document' could look like this:

1. Decide document is needed.
2. Switch on word processor.
3. Type document.
4. Merge data, e.g. address from Outlook address book if needed.
5. Save and name document.
6. Print document (if more than two pages).
7. Read document.
8. Correct mistakes on screen.
9. Finalise document.
10. Attach to e-mail and send to recipient.

Optional:

11. Print out hard copy and sign
12. Put in envelope and post

This very simple process can be undertaken in a variety of ways. For example, a more traditional approach in the law firm of yesteryear might have looked like this:

1. Decide document is needed.
2. Dictate document to tape.
3. Give tape to secretary.
4. Secretary types document.
5. Secretary prints document.
6. Secretary gives document to fee earner.
7. Fee earner reviews document and amends by hand.
8. Fee earner gives document back to secretary.
9. Secretary makes amendments.
10. Secretary prints document.
11. Secretary gives document to fee earner.
12. Loop round (7) to (11) as necessary.

13. Fee earner approves final document.
14. Secretary prints final copy of document.
15. Fee earner signs document.
16. Fee earner returns document to secretary.
17. Secretary produces envelope.
18. Secretary folds document and puts in envelope.
19. Secretary takes envelope to mail room.
20. Mail room weighs envelope.
21. Mail room franks envelope.
22. Mail room gets document collected.

As can be seen from the above example, technology and particularly use of the technology by the originator of the work, can cut down on the number of tasks to produce the final outcome of a posted letter.

In reality this rather simple example doesn't tell the whole story. It may well be that the second process is more efficient than the first for the simple reason that the fee earner's time is better spent dictating letters than in typing them, and few fee earners would disagree with that. However, the advantage of looking at things in this way is that it offers the opportunity for the analysis of what is actually going on.

While producing a document is a generic process across all law firms, doing business process analysis bottom-up, i.e. starting with the lowest level tasks, can become very confusing since the key is to understand how all the processes fit together. Because of this, process analysis usually adopts the top-down approach.

What is the top-down approach?

In essence this is a way of dividing up the work of a firm into a relatively few sets of high level processes. You then take these and break them down into smaller discrete processes and so on until you arrive at set of tasks that, if done in the correct sequence, will result in the desired outcome without having to understand the overall process.

In other words you look at dividing what you do into:

- business process
  - activities
    - tasks
      - sub-tasks.

It is probably not feasible to draw up a business process map for the whole of your practice, so you should look at the area of the firm where you have decided to place your e-business focus. This will be the area where you think integrating the Internet into what you do will bring greater client value.

There is no right way to divide up business processes, but Table 4.3 offers a starting point.

Table 4.3 Dividing up the business processes

Business process	Activities	Tasks/sub-tasks (in no particular order)
Marketing	Service defining Promoting Pricing Placing Relationship building	Attracting clients, either via traditional methods (advertising, word of mouth) or referral agencies (e.g. claims farms), providing general information related to the matter, cross-selling, inviting clients to seminars, sending them newsletters, etc.
Selling	Targeting Competing Persuading	Providing quotations, initial free legal advice sessions
Taking instructions	Interviewing Qualifying Accepting Checking Scoping Budgeting Referring	Initial interview, getting admin. details, assessing legal problem and costs. Advising on costs, getting up-front payments for disbursements, etc., filling in LSC forms
Matter planning	Analysing Strategising Managing Allocating Delegating	Client care letter, terms and conditions sent to client
Executing	Team working Meeting Negotiating Drafting Resourcing Researching Supervising Controlling Reporting Communicating	Doing the work. Document production, telephone calls, entering information into the practice management system, time recording, filing, etc. Appointing counsel and experts, supervising assistants and support staff, doing legal research, advising clients

Table 4.3 (*continued*)

Business process	Activities	Tasks/sub-tasks (in no particular order)
Completing	Billing Collecting Storing Reviewing Marketing	Final bill, archiving documents, sending relevant documents to client
Practice managing	Human resourcing	Recruiting, performance management, appraisal
	Financing	Managing the accounting and book keeping function, payroll, budgeting
	Procuring	Managing the purchase of goods and services for the firm including books, online legal resources, IT, stationery, utilities, telephone services
	IT	Managing the IT infrastructure
	Partnership	Providing information to partners, minutes of meetings, etc., planning

A very useful approach is to walk an imaginary client through your firm from beginning to end and define each activity/task that is undertaken to produce and deliver the service to them. There will be some processes that all clients go through regardless of matter type and others that are matter specific.

E-business opportunity analysis

In assessing what will really make a difference to what you are offering clients, you need to develop a list of the opportunities that exist. Here is a list to start you thinking:

- save time;
- improve communication;
- cut costs;
- build client loyalty;
- be more transparent;
- be more inclusive;
- personalise;
- make more convenient/reduce hassle;
- provide added value;
- make things easier;

- make things clearer;
- educate;
- delegate;
- improve quality;
- streamline;
- simplify.

Now look at the business processes you have defined and see where integrating the Internet will support the opportunity. At this stage it is useful to be as creative as possible and dream up some wild ideas to push the boundaries. You won't adopt all the ideas you come up with, but to really create competitive advantage you will need to be innovative, so allow yourself to think beyond what seems practical and reasonable right now.

Matching Internet possibilities to business processes: How do we know what we don't know?

A key source of frustration is that it's very hard to come up with new ideas when, as non-IT experts, you don't know what is possible using the technology. This naturally restricts creative thinking as you don't want to waste valuable fee earning time inventing something that can't work.

A pitfall

It is usually at this point that someone has the idea to go out into the market and see what's available. Then comes a series of sales pitches from various vendors of technology, and hey presto before you know it you end up implementing a system based on technology rather than the business. This is very easy to do and most law firms have done it at one point or another. The benefit is that you learn very quickly what's available. The downside is that you end up becoming technology – or more accurately vendor – driven, pulling you off the track of what you really wanted to achieve in the first place.

There is no easy answer to this; however, don't let it get in the way of imagination. If you have taken a little time to do some planning and research of what others are doing, you don't have to know the ins and outs of the technology to come up with a really useful and sound e-business design. Your design will be moulded and changed as you go through the implementation process. Table 4.4 offers some ideas.

Table 4.4 Business process opportunities

Opportunity	Process	How
Save time	Interviewing	Put up job descriptions on the Internet, have applicants apply online
	Taking instructions	Have a checklist to 'qualify' potential clients online Collect initial client data online in a pre-programmed form
	Doing the work	Have existing clients book their own appointments online as part of a client extranet
	Managing staff	Have leave forms filled in on the intranet and routed electronically to partner in charge for approval

Writing up business processes

There are many different formal schemas for representing business process models, including drawing flow charts and data models. At this stage the important thing is to write up what is proposed in such a way that others can be walked through the processes and evaluate them. Keep this to a few sides of A4.

IT infrastructure

For the purposes of this book IT infrastructure means the hardware, software and the way it's put together – configured – to deliver an e-business system. E-business relies on implementing sound and robust information technology systems that fully integrate the capabilities of the Internet into your business. It also goes without saying that what you intend to do needs to be integrated with your current IT systems and make use of what you already have.

Integration, integration, integration

Integration is mentioned a lot in the context of e-business because it is mission critical to any successful e-business operation. So what does this mean?

Integration happens on two different, interlinked levels.

- integration of working practices;
- integration of IT systems.

Integration of working practices

What this means is that the e-business element of what you are doing is designed to fit seamlessly with the way people work, and also involves looking at whether processes that were separate can be amalgamated by using the technology. This will often necessitate a different way of working and, as with any change, will take time to get right.

A very simple example, mentioned in Table 4.4, is using an intranet to enable staff to book leave. Previously staff may have had to fill in a paper form, and have it signed by their supervisor/partner who has to check that taking holiday at this time will not leave the department short of staff. This, in turn, involves checking what other leave is being taken at the same time. The form is then forwarded to whoever manages the leave/payroll in the firm and is finally confirmed. An intranet process would make this far simpler. The firm-wide leave diary is easily checked online; the form is filled in online and is automatically routed via e-mail to the relevant people, enabling a procedure that used to take days to be processed in minutes.

Integration of IT systems

Integrating IT systems – getting them to speak to each other and exchange information at the click of a button – has been the holy grail of the IT industry for many years and continues to be so with the Internet. In law firms, integration is a perennial problem.

Most law firms have implemented IT piecemeal resulting in islands of information held in different places. An example of this is where the conveyancing department operates a specialist case management system that is not fully integrated with the accounts system. This often means that client contact details are held in two separate places. The risk of this is that details are updated only in one place, and the resulting errors and confusion are easy to imagine. There are also issues around documents holding client information not being easy to find unless you know the precise place in which the information is held, for example who the mortgage lender is or the address of the property to be purchased.

However, there have been improvements with the advent of integrated practice management systems which have recently been developed by specialist legal IT suppliers. These have a client/matter database at their core with accounting, time record-ing, document production, diaries and scheduling and e-mail integrated to produce an electronic file. This level of integration makes the transition to e-business much easier. The cost of this kind of software has also become very reasonable in the past few years – fortunately the days of prohibitively expensive case man-agement systems are over. Visit **www.it.lawsociety.org.uk** to see a copy of the Law Society's annual *Software Solutions Guide* to find suppliers

A more in-depth look at IT components for e-business

In Chapter 2 we looked at the basic concepts and technologies in the Internet arena. This section is about how you might fit the jigsaw together to implement your e-business.

It is unlikely that you will be able to identify the exact tech-nical components you need to make your e-business work, as much of this will be down to the suppliers you eventually choose to work with and how they think it can best be implemented. But to give you some idea, Figure 4.3 illustrates a very simple ex-ample of an overall e-business IT infrastructure with the specific e-business components in capital letters.

There are many different configurations possible. Note that in the figure there is a specific person (info/web manager) in charge of managing and changing the structure and design of the website as opposed to just the content. To do this the manager will need the right tools to update the site. We shall explore each of these elements in more detail.

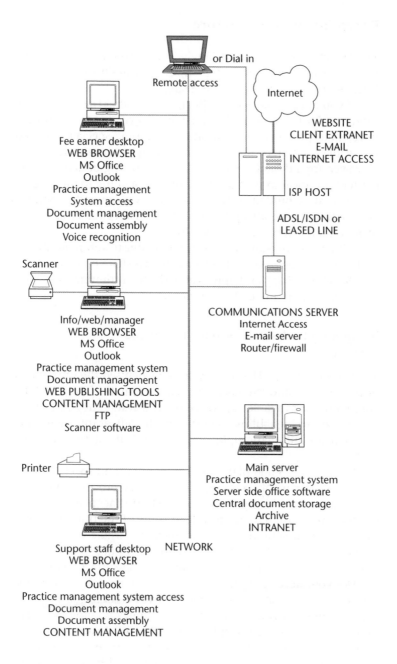

Figure 4.3 Components of an e-business IT infrastructure

Designing an infostructure

The last part of the design triangle is 'infostructure' which really refers to sources of the content that you intend to use on your intranet, extranet and public website.

If you already have a website, it is likely that the content you produced for it was either taken from your corporate brochure or developed specifically for the site. Developing specialist content is feasible for a static site that isn't going to change that often. However, for a dynamic e-business site, ongoing updating of site content is critical to success. If the site is not going to increase the administrative burden of the firm, then ways must be found to automatically generate updated content on a regular basis with as little human intervention as possible.

While it is not realistic to expect to be able to automate all content, it should be possible to ensure that the bare bones are available for easy editing and approval with the minimum of hassle.

This is where integration comes in.

Integrating back office systems to provide content

Most specialist legal IT suppliers have recognised the importance of the Internet and the need to make information from systems automatically available on websites. As a result they have been working on web-enabling their systems to deliver information in a format for automatic uploading to a website at the click of a button.

It is always a good plan to talk to your current specialist legal IT supplier as part of your e-business strategy process. Of course, they will want to lead you in the direction that their product is headed, but if you have done at least some of the thinking about the issues, you should be able to have a sensible conversation about what's possible with your current set-up. You will find more on selecting suppliers for your e-business in Chapter 6.

Do you need everything in-house to be fully integrated before you think about e-business? This is a good question and depends on what your final e-business strategy is going to be. For example, it would be possible to provide added value to clients simply by e-mailing a report to them every Friday on the status of their matter. This report could be generated by your current practice management system and would just require someone to e-mail this to each client in turn. This is not an integrated approach since it involves someone doing an additional task. However, you may decide that for some key clients it is worth doing and not having the process integrated and automated should not prevent you from doing it.

A more integrated approach could involve working with your practice management system supplier to see what could be achieved. The process could be changed so that you simply compile a list of the relevant clients from your database and then have an automated routine that sends out the report at the click of a button. This is technically feasible though dependent upon what your supplier is willing to do and at what cost.

The overall message is that the more integration you can achieve the better, and at the very least you should have some form of integrated practice management system in place before contemplating e-business. It is much easier to build on the firm foundation of integrated back and front office systems.

Document and knowledge management

Some law firms have document management systems and knowledge management systems. These terms can mean different things to different people. Like a lot of IT matters, it is easy to focus on the technology aspects and forget about the information part.

Knowing the difference between data, information and knowledge

Consider a managing partner looking at billed fees for the previous month. Raw data will simply comprise a set of amounts for each fee earner. Presented in the context of fees earned over previous months, or analysed according to matter type, the data then becomes information. Knowledge is knowing how to respond to the information and taking relevant action.

Knowledge is hard to define. In the context of a law firm, knowledge is what clients are paying for. Knowledge, however, stretches beyond an understanding of the law and how to apply it to all the various scenarios that clients present. It includes understanding practice, procedure, markets, how best to do things, such as understanding how a District Judge is likely to react, and a whole host of things in between.

Knowledge management systems

Knowledge management systems and tools are used to capture, re-use and re-purpose relevant information for the person who needs it, preferably at the right time. They can be as simple as a well organised set of precedents and templates, or as complex as a library of information resources drawn from a range of sources. These might include:

- online publishers;
- the firm's client documents catalogued in a way that shares knowledge;
- best practice manuals;
- newsletters;
- articles;
- white papers;
- counsel's opinions;
- e-mails from colleagues where pearls of wisdom have been captured in exchanges about previous cases.

It is highly likely that most of this information will be accessed through an intranet for internal use, with parts re-edited for client consumption on the client extranet or even on the public website. An example is articles that fee earners write on their specialism from time to time.

Outsourcing content production

You also have the option of using an external provider to source, develop and/or write copy for your website. Copy writing comes at various levels, from providing text for a brochureware website (which web designers can help you with) to outsourcing the production of client focused newsletters, e-marketing e-mails and more heavyweight content for your client extranet and public facing website. There are also organisations that will stream the latest news as text, audio and even video to your website, as well as various news clipping agencies that are willing to collate any type of information from all the major news sources (including trade magazines) and deliver it in electronic form. Starting points to find these suppliers include **www.lawzone.co.uk**

Risk management

Once you have completed your outline design, changes are likely as you start exploring how to implement it (see Chapter 6). It is essential that you spend some time thinking about the risks associated with what you are intending to do. Taking time to think about the risks means that you can amend your design accordingly and think through ways of minimising the risk – *before* you spend any money on it.

Analysing risks and threats

Key areas in which to assess impacts and risks are:

- *people* – i.e. who will be impacted and when?
- *processes* – i.e. what changes are going to be required to the way you work?
- *content* – i.e. what kind of information is going to be used/made available, where/how is it sourced (e.g. practice management system)?
- *technology* – what are the technological risks? For example, if you adopt the Internet into your way of working, what are the risks to the business if your link to the Internet goes down?
- *transactions* – what are the impact and risks associated with transactions with third parties, financial transactions, etc.?

Some very simple examples are listed in Table 4.5.

Table 4.5 Analysing risks and threats

Potential change area	Impact/risk	Who will be impacted?	Strategies to overcome risks
Improve internal administration – set up internal documents and office manual on a firm-wide intranet	Fee earning time lost in organising legal know-how Cost of training	Fee earners and support staff to develop documents	Ensure proper training Earmark fixed amount of fee earner time and manage this

Table 4.5 (*continued*)

Potential change area	Impact/risk	Who will be impacted?	Strategies to overcome risks
Set up online conveyancing service	Need more resources to handle the new traffic generated? Is the conveyancing department IT competent? Suspicion amongst support staff of IT	Conveyancing department	Ensure proper training Include department in design of system
Develop client extranet to improve transparency and service to clients	How will client information be kept updated? Can current IT system handle generating this automatically?	Whole firm (if extranet is for all clients)	Start with key clients and roll out to others later

Evaluating

So what is practical in terms of the risk that your firm will tolerate? Consider the potential change areas, the impact/risk of the change and the people who will be impacted. Take some time to think this through at a reasonably detailed level so that you have a clear idea of what the impact may really look like and take time to consider strategies to overcome the potential risks.

If you are an enthusiast about what you are intending to do, sometimes the temptation is not to consider risks, as these can be used as reasons not to implement the project. However, it is possible to use risk analysis to see if the benefits really do outweigh the risks. This type of analysis helps to root ideas in reality and ensures they are practical and achievable.

Building the business case

Once you have identified the opportunities to web-enable your practice, and thought through a strategy and design, an important next step is to build a business case to support the initiative to focus thinking further. A business case will be crucial to gaining support from the partnership. It also provides an opportunity to solidify the different concepts, budget and design in order to avoid costly mistakes. The content of the business case includes justification for the project, an assessment of the preliminary scope of the project and an assessment of the project's feasibility.

The business case provides justification for the project along strategic, operational, technical and financial lines, see Figure 4.4.

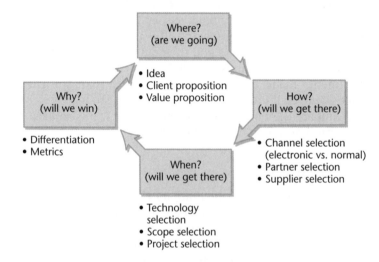

Figure 4.4 Key elements of a business case
Source: Kalakolta, R. and Robinson, M. (2001) *E-Business 2.0*, Addison-Wesley.

Key elements of a business case

*   *Strategic justification* – where are we going? This section of the business case outlines why you, as a firm, are doing this. What benefits (value) for clients and the firm will be achieved? How does it fit in with the firm's overall business plan? How does it fit in the competitive landscape?
*   *Operational justification* – how will we get there? This section of the plan identifies and quantifies the specific process improvements expected to result from integrating the Internet more closely into operations.

- *Technical justification* – when will we get there? This section identifies how the IT infrastructure will need to change and how this will contribute to improving operational efficiency or enable things to be done better and/or differently.
- *Financial justification* – why will we win? This section outlines the costs and benefits of the proposed new framework and quantifies these in terms meaningful to the firm.

Strategic justification and operational justification

It is sensible to discuss with key members of the firm what they would expect to see as key outcomes and what would constitute true benefit from their perspective. It is important to keep some focus on benefits to clients and then define benefits to the firm, as often these discussions can end up internally focused with adjustments made that suit the firm rather than the clients. While the overall intention of any e-business strategy is to positively impact the bottom line of the firm, it works to keep the client firmly in the middle of the picture.

Technical justification

If you have undertaken a preliminary IT infrastructure analysis, then you will know what hardware and software you have in place that can support your plan. You will also have identified the gaps but it may be that you won't know exactly what is needed to fill them. Be assured that this is not some technical failing on your part. In developing a technical justification you will need to talk to vendors so you can start to get a fix on what is available in the market, and more importantly what will be the likely cost.

Financial justification

The core of any business case is a cost/benefit analysis in the context of business needs.

The cost/benefit analysis issue

Back in the 1980s and early 1990s there was a myth that IT purchases could be justified on the basis of a straightforward cost/benefit analysis. The problem with this approach was that while the tangible costs were very obvious, the benefits were harder to define and were often things like improved efficiency, faster document turnaround and other unmeasurable items. While it is patently true that a word processor is a more efficient way of producing a document than a typewriter, measuring the benefits with any degree of accuracy to enable a straight monetary value to be given has proven almost impossible.

However, the analysis is still a very useful exercise in obtaining clarity around expected benefits and likely costs. It does not have to be a lengthy document, as the process of development, i.e. thinking it through with others is as important as the final document. Table 4.6 provides an example. Hard benefits are measured in financial terms. Benefits that contribute to operations can be considered soft benefits, not measurable in financial terms.

Table 4.6 Cost/benefit analysis

Business need	Incremental costs	Soft benefits	Hard benefits
Increase client satisfaction through being more transparent	Hardware and software costs ISP costs Consultancy costs	To improve competitiveness More word of mouth referrals To be recognised as market leader in the field	More fee income Opportunity to charge subscriptions for detailed information

A generic list of benefits to help you think this through is given in Table 4.7.

Table 4.7 Tangible and intangible benefits

Tangible benefits	Intangible benefits
Increased fees through: • new clients sourced online • existing clients (cross-selling) • being able to report more effectively to bulk referrers • being able to handle more work through improved business processes taking less time	Firm's image Enhancing 'brand' More rapid, more responsive marketing communications Faster turnaround on legal work Improved client care Learning for the future Meeting client expectations of a professional presence on the web

Table 4.7 (*continued*)

Tangible benefits	Intangible benefits
Marketing cost reductions from: • reduced number of client queries • reduced printing and distribution • cost of marketing communications Supply-chain cost reductions from: • reduced time for legal research • quicker turnaround on searches, counsel consultation, etc. • CPD point training online Administrative cost reductions from: • more efficient routine business processes, e.g. recruitment, online ordering of stationery, invoice payment, holiday authorisation, etc.	Identifying new partners (e.g. bulk referrers), supporting existing partners better (e.g. counsel, other third parties) Better management of marketing information and client information Feedback from clients on services

Show us the money: revenue models

Don't forget that there are opportunities for generating income from online activities. Here are some revenue models currently being used in the legal market:

- subscriptions (to documents/library or an updating newsletter);
- pay-per-view or download of documents (i.e. each document is sold for a one-off price);
- advertising from third party providers;
- panel fees from third party providers;
- update payments – documents are provided free for a certain time after which users are encouraged to pay for updates;
- service charge added to fees (for use of extranet for example);
- fixed fee payment for initial advice – users are provided with a diagnosis for a fixed fee.

Don't forget that if you intend to take online payments there will be additional costs in setting up a secure infrastructure for taking credit card payments. This is not as complex as you might think – most ISPs will be able to help you with this, or for handling invoicing and credit control offline.

Cost analysis

The starting point is to estimate the costs associated with implementing the new system. Likely costs are:

- hardware;
- software;
- services (one-time consultancy, website development, integration with current systems, training and testing);
- support and maintenance (including ongoing systems administration, hosting services from ISP, support, etc.);
- staff and fee earning time.

Savings analysis

Once you understand the specific costs, the next goal is to measure the savings related to the implementation of the new plan. Do this in two stages, comparing the costs of doing it the way you do it now with the expected costs once the new system is in place. These will be estimates and it is prudent to overestimate costs and underestimate savings. It has to be said that this is not a very precise science and its usefulness probably lies more in the process of working it through and gaining fresh insights into what will work, rather than the final figures that you come up with.

Assessing costs

Working out what everything is going to cost when you are not clear exactly what is needed is a difficult task. It's back to the old chestnut 'how do we know what we don't know'? There are various approaches to this, from hiring an IT consultant through talking to your current vendors to get some ideas of costs. At best it will be very imprecise, but the intention at this stage is to enable you to start thinking about what level of budget you need to set to make it happen, with a view to avoiding nasty shocks at partnership meetings.

Setting an e-business budget

Law firms often tackle the issue of budgeting by tendering to vendors first and then setting the budget based on the best bid received. While this is not a bad idea, setting financial limits that are agreed at the outset, enables a smoother implementation process.

Tips and tricks for e-business strategy

Smart things to avoid. Don't:

- underestimate the amount of work required in the firm for the solution to work;
- forget to look at how others in the legal market are doing it;
- build a strategy that is not based around core business;
- try to 'boil the ocean' by including too many functions all at once;
- do little or no research on the impact of the change in your firm;
- try to sell the idea to the partnership by underestimating the costs;
- forget to include change management in the thinking;
- sell the system internally without a supporting business case;
- hope that new working practices will start when the new system is implemented;
- become transfixed by the technology alone. It should support a clearly defined business need.

Smart things to implement. Do:

- ensure that all the partners have 'bought into' the ideas;
- involve everyone who is going to be impacted (including support staff);
- make sure that those involved have an understanding of the technology and the way the firm may have to change to support it;
- focus on high-return, high-profile opportunities;
- think outside the box in coming up with ideas;
- develop and agree a budget by whatever means;
- document the business case;
- develop a phased approach – don't try to do it all at once.

Notes

1   Quoted from Cunningham, M. (2002), *Smart Things to Know About E-business*, Capstone.
2   Susskind, R. (1996) *The Future of Law*, OUP.

5

Designing e-business websites

Websites are the core of e-business activity. The topic is huge and there are many good books on the subject that look at websites from a wide perspective ranging from the very technical to the strategic as marketing tools.[1] For the purpose of this book our focus will be on using websites as the main vehicle to deliver e-business capability, which, as we have seen, is about integrating the Internet into your day-to-day working and leveraging what it can do to provide new and additional value to your clients and to your firm's business processes. We will look at the different uses to which websites can be put and outline principles for good design.

Intranets, extranets and public websites

There are three classes of website which are defined more or less by the type of user who has access to them:

- the intranet;
- the extranet;
- the public website.

As intranets, extranets and public websites all use the same technology and standards it does not make sense to operate them as three completely separate entities. Often content that is useful for the intranet, is also appropriate in a slightly different form for a client extranet or even the public website. It makes sense to think of intranets, extranets and websites as one entity using the same infrastructure, but having different users. See Figure 5.1.

The public website

Only one third of law firms in England and Wales currently have a website. Some of the most frequently cited reasons for not having one are:

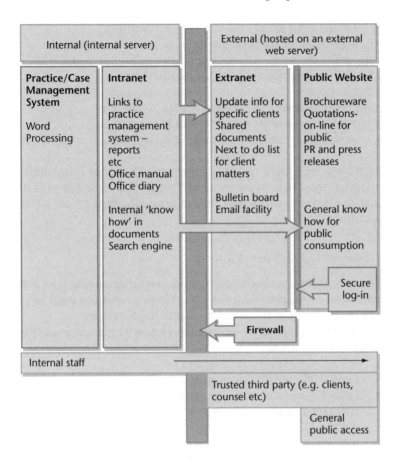

Figure 5.1 How intranet, extranet and a public website infrastructure can fit together

- We don't see the point – we have never been convinced that a marketing leaflet online will get us new business.
- We have enough problems getting our ordinary IT systems sorted out, without getting involved in the Internet.
- Most of our clients or likely clients don't use the Internet anyway.
- Our clients wouldn't be interested in our website.
- It seems like it could become another way to waste money on IT for very little return.
- We've now got e-mail and that will do for the time being.

- I think it's a good idea, but my partners don't.
- We've just never thought about it.

Most of these reasons can be summarised as:

- lack of foreseeable tangible benefit to the firm;
- lack of foreseeable tangible benefit for clients;
- perceived complexity of making it happen.

These are legitimate responses since it's often not immediately apparent what benefit a website will bring. This, coupled with the hassle of implementing one, leaves firms wondering whether it's worth the bother.

Stages of website development

There is no doubt that some firms do feel that having a website has value – as can be seen from a review of what the legal world is already doing in the arena of online legal services.

Traditional stages of website development are (adapted from Chaffey et al., 2000[2]):

- *Level 0*. No website or presence on the web.
- *Level 1*. Basic web presence. Firm places an entry in a website listing company such as **www.yell.co.uk** to make people aware of the existence of the firm and its services. There is no website at this stage.
- *Level 2*. Simple static informational website. Contains basic firm and service information – the brochureware site.
- *Level 3*. Simple interactive site. Users are able to search the site and make queries to retrieve information, such as online quotations and online calculators. Queries by e-mail may also be supported.
- *Level 4*. Interactive site supporting transactions with users. The functions will vary according to the firm. They will usually be limited to some form of online buying, for example, subscribing for information or purchasing documents.
- *Level 5*. Fully interactive site supporting the client (and/or supplier interactions). Provides relationship management with individual clients through matter management and develops an ongoing relationship with clients (client extranet/virtual deal room, etc.).

Effective e-business websites are at level 4 or 5 and an as yet undefined level 6 is emerging where there is seamless integration (seamless *and* secure) between the internal processes of the firm and its environment. This is the true 'virtual' organisation, where the physical boundaries of the firm cease to have any real meaning from the point of view of the client.

Principles of good website design

Good user-centred design starts with an understanding of the nature and variation within the user groups. According to Bevan[3] the following issues are to be considered:

- Who are the important users?
- Why do they access the site?
- How frequently will they visit the site?
- What experience and expertise do they have?
- What nationality are they – do they speak English?
- What type of information are they looking for?
- How will they want to use the information: read it on the screen, print it or download it?
- What type of browsers will they use?
- How fast will their communications links be?
- How large a screen/window will they use with how many colours?

An example of customer orientation in action can be seen in B&Q's DIY site (**www.diy.com**). This is targeted at a range of users of DIY products so the site has three zones: products, advice and inspiration. Experts who know what they want can go straight to product listings, whereas less experienced people can get advice as they would in a store. Finally, beginners can go to the inspiration section where they can see room mock-ups with lists of the products needed to create a particular look. While the content of this site is obviously not applicable to law firms, the concept of providing for different levels of users is a good one.

In thinking this through for clients, an idea (suggested by Bevan) is to define key scenarios and then interview potential users and walk them through the scenarios using some sort of mock-up of what is being proposed.

Do you need more than one website?

Some law firms have adopted the approach of having a brochure-ware website for the firm, and another website dedicated to a specific area or set of clients they want to work with. Each site may have a completely different look and feel to reflect the concerns of the separate intended audiences.

This can be a good approach as it means the site can be 'owned' by the department responsible for that area of work. If they see it as an extension of the services offered to their particular set of clients there is more incentive to keep it relevant and fresh.

For every website you will need a separate domain name if it is to be referenced directly (e.g. **www.only-family-law.co.uk**) over the web.

CASE STUDY   **Web accessibility**

The topic of making your website accessible to a whole range of users is about to become a matter of law and clearly something that firms need to be thinking about.

Disability Discrimination Act 1995

The Disability Discrimination Act 1995 aims to end the discrimination which many disabled people face and gives disabled people rights in the areas of:

- employment
- buying or renting land or property
- access to goods, facilities and services.

The employment rights and first rights of access came into force on 2 December 1996; further rights of access came into force on 1 October 1999; and the final rights of access are due to come into force in October 2004. This final stage means that service providers will have to make permanent physical adjustments to their premises by the above date.

It is widely recognised within the IT industry that the above provisions of the Disability Discrimination Act will include equal access to electronic information and services, in the same way that physical access to facilities/premises is required.

Various organisations have worked to develop accessibility codes of practice applying specifically to websites to satisfy the legal imperative.

The W3C and the WAI

Chief amongst these are the World Wide Web Consortium's (**www.w3.org**) (W3C) sponsored body: the Web Accessibility Initiative (**www.w3.org/WAI/**) (WAI).

In co-ordination with other organisations around the world, they have developed a set of universal standards to ensure compliance. These are called the *Web Content Accessibility Guidelines 1.0 (WCAG 1.0).*

The standards

The majority of these guidelines are aimed at securing proper provision for the visually and aurally impaired, as well as users with motor neurone disabilities. With the advent of alternative browsers, 'speaking browsers', Braille readers and text recognition software, disabled users are now able to access information via the Internet easily – if websites observe the WCAG 1.0 guidelines and are written in correct HTML.

These guidelines provide three levels or priorities of compliance:

- Priority 1. Web content *must* satisfy this checkpoint. Otherwise, one or more groups will find it impossible to access information in the document. Satisfying this checkpoint is a basic requirement for some groups to be able to use web documents.
- Priority 2. Web content *should* satisfy this checkpoint. Otherwise, one or more groups will find it difficult to access information in the document. Satisfying this checkpoint will remove significant barriers to accessing web documents.
- Priority 3. Web content *may* address this checkpoint. Otherwise, one or more groups will find it somewhat difficult to access information in the document. Satisfying this checkpoint will improve access to web documents.

When must firms comply by?

The UK government is currently taking this issue very seriously and has stated in their own *Guidelines for Government Websites* that all future government sites must conform to a minimum of level 1 of the WCAG 1.0 guidelines, and that existing sites be gradually 'retro-fitted' to incorporate these checkpoints. This was announced by the then E-government Minister Ian McCartney at the E-communicators Conference, 1 February 2001.

All non-government sites must conform to level 1 compliance by October 2004. Although this deadline may seem distant, exist-ing sites which continue to develop in a non-compliant way (or newly commissioned sites which do not incorporate the WCAG 1.0 checkpoints) are building on poor foundations and later 'retro-fitting' may well be more costly.

In 2004, who will be held legally liable should a complaint against a website lead to legal action?

This may be complex – particularly in cases where one organi-sation commissions another to produce and manage a website on their behalf. The Code of Practice published in conjunction with the Disability Discrimination Act suggests that it is the site owner who would be held to have prime responsibility for its legality. So ulti-mately it is the responsibility of each organisation to comply with legal requirements in so far as they affect its own operations.

As well as satisfying the legal requirement, conformance with the WCAG 1.0 guidelines will actually enhance the market share and audience reach of your website by increasing its general usability.

It can be argued that adoption of the WCAG 1.0 recommen-dations demonstrates a commitment to social responsibility and equity of access to information and services. In addition, many of the WCAG 1.0 checkpoints will directly improve the performance of web services and reduce the maintenance effort required.

www.ontheslate.com

Designing a client oriented site

A well designed site will be oriented towards your clients. This involves the difficult task of trying to provide content and ser-vices that appeal to a wide range of clients. This is where having segmented your clients into groups (see Chapter 4) comes in use-ful as it will enable you to profile them more effectively. As noted above, there exists the temptation to categorise your clients by their matter type and design a website accordingly, for example by setting up a family law area or a probate area. In essence there is nothing wrong with this, but it is not really a client oriented approach – since clients don't often see themselves as a family matter, more often as someone who is trying to solve a domestic crisis. The distinction is subtle, but if thought through can profoundly affect the way you design and present your site.

As well as client groups designers also need to take account of variations in the backgrounds of visitors to the site. These can be thought of in terms of different types of familiarity:

- *familiarity with the Net* – are shortcuts provided for those familiar with the Net? And for novices is there help to lead them through the site?
- *familiarity with the organisation* – for clients who don't know the firm, content is needed to explain who you are and to demonstrate credibility through an 'About Us' option.
- *familiarity with your services* – even existing clients may not know the full range of your services. You need a way of presenting these that appears relevant to them.
- *familiarity with your site* – site maps, search and help options are important to ensure that clients do not get frustrated with your site and refuse to visit it.

Dynamic design and personalisation

Internet-based personalisation delivers customised content and services for the individual user of the website. There are three distinct approaches:

- *customisation* – this allows users to visit the site and set up their specific preferences.
- *individualisation* – this goes beyond the fixed setting of customisation and uses patterns of the visitor's own behaviour (known because of a unique log-in ID) to deliver specific content that follows their patterns of contact.
- *group characterisation* – the visitor receives recommendations based on groups of 'similar' people via collaborative filtering and case-based reasoning.

Elements of site design

Having established the requirements of the users and potential users, the next thing to consider is how they will interact with the website. There are three broad elements to this:

- *site design and structure* – the overall structure of the site;
- *page design* – the layout of the individual pages;
- *content design* – how the text and graphic content on each page is designed.

Site design and structure

The structures developed by designers will vary a great deal, and in essence this is what you are paying them for – to come up with something that is meaningful and useful to your clients. A description of the key elements follows.

Site style

An effective website design will have an overall look and feel through the use of colour, images, typefaces, fonts and layout that is consistent with your 'brand'.

Site personality

The style elements can be combined to develop a distinct personality for your site. You can describe site personalities in the same way that you describe people, for example, formal or fun. An example of a site where this has been thought about is **www.egg.com**.

Site organisation

This is concerned with how you intend to categorise the information you are presenting. As has been outlined above, the usual way with legal sites is to do it by matter type. Other ways include breaking it down by topic, task or audience. The use of metaphors or icons is also common, for example Microsoft Windows Explorer uses the metaphors of files in folders and trash in bins that mirror the real world. The use of a shopping basket metaphor is common on e-commerce sites. However, metaphors can be confusing if they are not instantly understood.

Site navigation schemes

Devising a site that is easy to use is critically dependent on the design of the site navigation scheme. This is really about 'flow' or how easy it is for a user to find the information they need on the site and it also includes actions such as completing on-site forms. A common rule of thumb is the three-click rule: it shouldn't take more than three mouse clicks to find the relevant information once the user has entered the site.

On large sites the three-click rule may end up with the home page looking cluttered. One approach to this is to develop a series of home pages for different user groups (see above).

It is also necessary to compromise on the amount of space taken up by menus and navigation bars since there needs to be as much room as possible given over to content (Nielson, 2000).[4]

Page design

Page design is about creating an appropriate layout for each page. The main elements of any page are title, navigation and content. Issues in page design include the following.

Page elements

The proportion of the page devoted to content must be balanced with all the other material such as headers, footers, and navigation elements. It is conventional for main menus to be at the top or on the left.

Frames

Framed pages are generally discouraged for the following reasons:

- Search engines do not index them as well as non-frame sites so the site may appear lower down the search engine listings than competitor sites. (Search engines are discussed in more detail in Chapter 7.)
- Frames make it difficult to measure the number of page impressions (a page impression is one person viewing one site) on the site. Each frame counts as one page impression the first time the home page is loaded although the user is only viewing one page.
- Frames make it difficult to bookmark or print pages since it is not always clear which frame is to be bookmarked or printed.
- Frames are marginally slower to load than non-frame sites.

- Frames can't accommodate accessibility options, e.g. speaking browsers (see the case study on web accessibility above).

Resizing

A good page layout should allow the user to change the size of the text or work with different monitor resolutions.

Consistency

Page layout should be similar for all areas of the site. Standards of colour and typography can be enforced through a technique known as cascading style sheets.

Printing

Layout should allow for printing or provide an alternative printing format.

Content design

Copywriting for the web is evolving into an art form, but many of the rules for writing good copy are the same as for any media. Common errors on websites are:

- Too much knowledge is assumed of the visitor about the firm or legal services in general.
- The use of legal jargon and assumptions that clients will understand matter types, specialist types of documents and forms and legal process and procedure.
- Strange, inappropriate or irrelevant graphics. Legal websites abound with these, with one law firm's site having the graphic of a neatly arranged set of headstones for their probate section. There is also an overabundant use of legal visual clichés, for example scales of justice, wig and pen, quills, scrolls and leather bound books – not appropriate for a profession that is updating itself in the electronic age.
- Self-referential material. Content that sounds self-congratulatory (watch partner profiles here) and pictures of your very nice Georgian high street premises can make you appear pompous and patronising if not handled appropriately.

- Too glossy. In web terms this means designing a site that is 'flashtastic' (the overuse of Flash animation). Flash is great for creating an instant impression, but rapidly becomes boring when you've seen the animation more than once. Avoid having busy graphics scooting across the screen and distracting attention from the main purpose of the site – which must always be to present content.

Given the general public's impression of solicitor's firms, it is vital to think this through. The aim is to appear competent, professional and friendly – not an easy combination, and one that requires some careful thought.

It is also important to remember that a lot of the information will be read on screen. Approaches that can help deal with the limitations of using a monitor include the following:

- writing more concisely than in brochures;
- chunking text, or breaking it into units of five or six lines at most, which allows users to scan rather than read information on web pages;
- using lists with headline text in larger fonts;
- not including too much on a single page, except when presenting lengthy information such as a report which may be easier to read on one page;
- using hyperlinks to decrease page sizes or help achieve flow within copy, either by linking to sections further down the page or to other pages.

Keep clients coming back: push and pull

When thinking through the initial design of your website, it is important to consider how you will keep your users informed about the site. Websites are defined as 'pull' as they need to pull users to them, that is the user decides when and how often they will log on. In the 'push' process, where you alert the user to something – usually via e-mail, the user is passive and does not have a choice about receiving the information. They do, of course have a big choice about whether they read it or not, but that's another matter.

More discussion on this topic will be found in Chapter 7 on e-marketing.

Intranets

Intranets are the unsung heroes of what web technologies make available. As they become more sophisticated in what they can do, they are also starting to evolve into corporate or enterprise portals, that is, they act as a portal or gateway to information that is relevant to everyone in the firm and they can also help the individual manage their information resources. Specialist software is emerging for the development of intranet/portal type applications. See the Case Study for further information.

CASE STUDY   **Portals definitions**

'Portal' is a term, generally synonymous with 'gateway', for a World Wide Web site that is or proposes to be a major starting site for users when they get connected to the Web or that users tend to visit as an anchor site. There are general portals and specialised or niche portals. Some major general portals include Yahoo!, Excite, Netscape, Lycos, CNET, Microsoft Network and America Online's AOL.com. Examples of niche portals include Garden.com (for gardeners), Fool.co.uk (for investors) and SearchNetworking.com (for network administrators). In the legal world Venables.co.uk as well as the sites offered by the legal publishers, Sweet & Maxwell, Lawtel, Butterworths and Westlaw are some examples.

A number of large access providers offer portals to the Web for their own users. Most portals have adopted the Yahoo! style of content categories with a text-intensive, faster loading page visitors will find easy to use and to return to. Companies with portal sites have attracted much stock market investor interest because portals are viewed as able to command large audiences and numbers of advertising viewers.

Typical services offered by portal sites include a directory of websites, a facility to search for other sites, news, weather information, e-mail, stock quotes, phone and map information, and sometimes a community forum. Excite is among the first portals to offer users the ability to create a site that is personalised for individual interests.

Enterprise information portal

The enterprise information portal (EIP), or corporate portal, is a concept for a website that serves as a single gateway to a company's information and knowledge base for employees and possibly for customers, business partners and the general public as well.

In one model, an EIP is made up of the following elements: access/search, categorisation, collaboration, personalisation, expertise and profiling, application integration and security.

- *Access/search.* Access/search allows a user to get all the information needed (but no more) in the desired context. For example, a loan officer does not need marketing information to approve a loan. An EIP makes sure the loan officer gets only the information needed. In the legal world this translates as a probate fee earner not being presented with conveyancing information, for example.
- *Categorisation.* An EIP categorises all information so that it is delivered to the user within the context needed. In the legal world, this means the subject headings are relevant to the fee earner/support staff.
- *Collaboration.* An EIP allows individuals to collaborate regardless of geographical location. For example, criminal practitioners, with suitable mobile equipment, can collaborate with their support staff at the office or with counsel.
- *Personalisation.* The information provided to individuals using an EIP is personalised to that person's role, preferences and habits.
- *Expertise and profiling.* Expertise and profiling is essential for the collaboration element of an EIP. Individuals within an enterprise are profiled according to their experience and competencies. If individuals need to collaborate with others, they can choose those who are qualified for the project.
- *Application integration.* This allows individuals to deliver, access and share information regardless of applications used.
- *Security.* This provides information to users based on security clearance. The user logs on and is given access only to information that the user is authorised to access.

www.whatis.com

Using intranets as a standard desktop

It is likely that you have a range of different applications that you use from day to day. These might include the following:

- Windows Explorer or My Computer or Network Neighbour-hood for finding folders and files (documents) on the central server;
- Microsoft Office:
  - Word
  - Outlook (for e-mail, diary, rudimentary contacts)
  - Excel (spreadsheet)
  - Powerpoint (for presentations);
- specialist legal software:
  - accounts and time recording package and/or
  - practice management system and/or
  - case management system;
- larger firm applications:
  - document management system – replacing the need to use Windows and/or Word to find documents;
  - know-how system – some way of accessing templates, precedents and other documents via search facilities, which usually incorporates some form of document management system;
- online legal resources, which may be part of the know-how system:
  - either stored on the internal network, taken from CDs or the central server
  - or accessed directly from the Internet;
- other popular applications including:
  - document assembly tools (Ghostfill, HotDocs)
  - voice recognition
  - general Internet access.

Imagine if these were all integrated into a single interface: you switch on your computer in the morning and it takes you directly to your firm's intranet home page viewed through your web browser.

The first thing that appears on your screen is a list of your appointments for the day, together with legal news headlines of direct interest to the type of work that you do, and you can get the full story from the information source on the Internet, for example the legal section of *The Times*. All of the above applications are available through the web browser and organised in a way that makes sense to you – you are only ever three clicks away from getting to the heart of what you want to be doing.

Coupled with this, a whole host of other useful information is available, such as the firm's telephone and extension directory, the office manual, leave and other forms, stationery request forms – in fact all the internal administrative paperwork in an easy-to-use format. You can fill in forms online and automatically route them to the relevant person in the firm. Leave requests, sick leave forms, travel booking requests get sent via e-mail to the right person at the click of a button. There is a staff bulletin board where people post items they've got for sale or invitations to social events, saving the need to clutter already overburdened inboxes with e-mail. The firm-wide diary is available for everyone to see, together with the latest update on key clients, the firm's client newsletters, even a warning list of clients who are on the warpath and need kid-glove treatment when they next call in. In fact anything and everything that supports everyone in the firm to get the job done.

There is a list of your favourite legal research website links, that you can search by key word – getting information only from those sites – thus eliminating all the junk that results from a normal Internet search and saving hours of frustrating legal research time. You can seamlessly (and safely) link from the internal intranet onto the web at a single click and include and exclude legal source material sites at will. You can also search across all your internal as well as external resources by key word and bring up a mix of internal documents that have already been produced on a topic as well as material from external websites for your perusal. You can download information that is of interest to you and store it in a much more meaningful and sensible way than the favourites folder in your web browser currently makes possible, so you can read it later or get your support person to print it off for you to read on the train on the way home.

The point is that everything you are likely to need for your day-to-day work, including internal administration is in one easy to find and use place, organised around the way you and your firm works, rather than the way the system works.

However, as with everything that's worthwhile, all this takes a time to set up. Many specialist legal software suppliers are now working on this kind of vision and starting to make their software web-enabled so that it can be employed in this way.

The intranet as a starting point

Setting up an intranet is a particularly useful exercise for firms that are new to the idea of e-business and want to put a toe (or leg!) in the water to experiment with what's possible. An intranet provides the perfect vehicle for online form filling in all sorts of guises including everything from leave requests to travel booking requirements and so on. It can also provide a seamless link to your list of chosen suppliers' websites and you can start to order online.

Intranets are particularly useful for making office manuals, policies and procedures accessible and user friendly. Given that you can design these types of documents as web pages so they have hypertext capability and graphics, they instantly become more useable and accessible to everyone in the firm with a PC and web browser.

Intranets are also a useful tool for disseminating training information and are particularly good at providing just-in-time training support via 'How To' sheets and a 'Frequently Asked Questions' file.

As we have seen, intranets are set up in a very similar way to public websites, the only difference being that they are hosted internally, that is they run on your network's own server. Many firms buy a separate server for their intranet and run it almost exactly as they would an external web server.

Extranets

Client extranets are one method of demonstrating client care through transparency. However, a very good way to produce a collective shudder amongst solicitors is to suggest giving clients direct access to their matter records. This instantly brings up the picture of clients roving around the firm's internal network stumbling across the 'true' story. In reality, the information contained in client extranets is usually only summary information, drawn from a practice or case management system, posted onto the external website on a regular basis. There is no danger of clients being let loose in your electronic filing cabinets. It is very likely that your e-business will rely heavily on developing a useful client extranet if the focus of your strategy is on your clients.

Designing a client extranet

As extranets are simply websites with restricted access they should follow good website design principles. Being externally facing it is extremely important that they present the right information, at the right time, in an easy to use and attractive way.

Behind the scenes a client extranet will be based on a database, and use active server page technologies. This is because the nature of the information you are offering is dynamic, i.e. it changes, sometimes hourly. Managing this effectively is only possible through the use of a database and ASP pages.

Distinguishing features of an extranet include the provision of a log-in ID (user name) and password. The most secure way of managing this to make sure that only the people you intend to visit the site gain access, is for you to allocate a user name and password and send this to your client. You might give your users the facility to change their user names and passwords once they have logged into the extranet. It is important that the client has agreed at the outset to have their information made available in this way.

The client extranet can either be part of your public website – with a separate log-in area for your clients – or be a completely separate site, hosted by a different provider. For example, some specialist legal software vendors provide a client extranet design and hosting facility either as a bespoke development for your firm or as an application service provision solution, i.e. you rent the facilities rather than buy them.

So what does a client extranet look like?

As outlined above, a client extranet presents personalised information to the client when they log into the client extranet area. They have access only to their own records and it is impossible for them to see other clients' records by mistake.

The range of information you can present to your clients really only depends on what you want them to see and what you can readily make available to them in the correct (HTML) format. As discussed in Chapter 3, typical functionality and content includes:

- matter reporting (status tracking);
- financial reporting;
- online archives;
- online project management;
- online case management.

Other functions that can be included are:

- hosting online events (e.g. web seminars) for clients;
- the latest news about your firm and other items that will be of interest to clients;
- links to other resources that clients might find useful (including sites such as Amazon for books);
- the ability for clients to update their own personal and matter information that is held in the practice/case management system.

The key deciders are what will provide most value to your clients.

Levels of client extranet

It is helpful to think of client extranets at three levels:

- *Reporting* – those that seek to provide passive updates on client matters (one-way reporting with e-mail facilities). Clients log in and view progress on their matter.
- *Interactive* – those that seek to provide a more interactive environment to engage with clients: reporting, document sharing, bulletin board for shared conversations and e-mail for private conversations. This type of extranet can also incorporate 'push', i.e. sending e-mails to the client desktop when something is added to the extranet that they will be interested in seeing.
- *Collaborative* – those that provide a collaborative working environment: virtual deal room facilities including all of the above, together with shared project management facilities, document amendment and version control, full document storage and library facilities (i.e. searching and annotation) and shared diaries.

Tips and tricks for client extranets

- The starting point is to identify a discrete set of clients for whom an extranet will provide added value to both them and the firm. Don't try to be all things to all clients.
- Make sure that you have a procedure for clients to quickly get their password if they forget it (this can be automated via e-mail).
- Start small with a few valuable clients and ask them what they would like. If you ask the questions you must be prepared for the answers. So if they ask for a running record of costs, hours spent so far and likely bills, you must be prepared to give this information.
- Keep the initial design as simple as possible, adhering to the three-click rule – it should not take more than three clicks to get from the home page to the piece of information being sought.
- Keep the content simple, but useful. The temptation is to give out either too little or too much. Summary reports in the key areas of interest to clients are more useful than a set of milestones that they don't understand, or masses of Word documents – unless you are developing a virtual archive or deal room.
- If your client is a company have their logo appear on each page of their information as well as your firm's logo. This will give a feeling of partnership.
- Don't forget to build in features that will enhance client loyalty – see Chapter 7 on e-marketing.
- Be clear where the client information is going to come from and how much additional work will be required to get it into the extranet. The ideal situation is to set up your practice/case management system in such a way that the information can be published to the extranet at the click of a button – these systems do exist. Having a well organised intranet with facilities to publish to the web will also be a major contribution to keeping the extranet fed and happy.
- Have a panic button that means you can instantly take down information as well as put it up – this is for those times (and they will happen) when mistakes are made and wrong/unsuitable material is posted to the extranet.
- Design in some 'push' features, either by SMS or e-mail. Make sure that clients and other users are reminded on a frequent

basis about the existence of the extranet and the benefits it can provide for them.

Documenting your website design

Table 5.1 provides a checklist that you can use to design your e-business. You can download a copy of this from **www. opportunity-consulting.co.uk.**

Table 5.1 Documenting your website design

Task/item	Commentary and examples
IT infrastructure	
Does everyone have a networked PC?	This is a prerequisite for a successful intranet Getting a well managed and robust network and IT infrastructure together is a prerequisite for any e-business activity
Does everyone have a web browser and Internet access?	You do not have to have Internet access to operate a successful intranet, however, the usefulness of an intranet is increased exponentially if linked to the Internet
Do you have any home workers or people who want to be able to log in to your internal system from home or on the road?	These issues can be handled as part of upgrading your internal network if required
Do you want to connect branches or update your current connection?	
Do you have a security infrastructure?	Your network should have a firewall separating it from the Internet. If you are not clear what security measures are in place, talk to your network managers/external suppliers You should also have a general security policy (see Chapter 6 on implementation)
Intranet server	
If you are setting up an intranet where will you run it from – is there room on your current server?	The usual approach for setting up an intranet is to run it on a separate server (computer)

Table 5.1 (*continued*)

Task/item	Commentary and examples
ISP/hosting Who hosts your current website?	If you already have Internet e-mail you will have a relationship with an ISP. They will very likely also host websites. However, it may pay to shop around. See Chapter 6 on implementation
Do you have a domain name?	Have you registered a relevant name for your firm, e.g. **www.myfirm.co.uk**?
Website Who are the primary audience for your website(s)?	Clients? Staff? General public? Suppliers? Other stakeholders?
Will you have a single website for both public and client extranet or will you have two sites (more accurately two home pages referenced by two separate domain names)?	Some firms have completely separate domain names and separate websites for each area, e.g. one website for their employment law clients and another for their family law clients
What works about your current website? What do you think needs to be changed?	Using the guidelines on good website design above, do you think your current website needs to be redesigned in any way?
Describe in general terms how your website will be structured for your intended audience. (Check Chapter 3 for what's possible and what other law firms are doing)	*Example:* Client extranet As part of our initial client care procedures we will send the client a unique user name and password. When they log in they will be able to see the following information: • initial instructions form where they can fill in their own details about their matter; • a checklist showing how far the matter has progressed; • a list of outstanding tasks; • the fees that we expect to charge including disbursements; • all relevant documents as Word files, etc. There will also be a general news area and the ability to purchase DIY documents online

Table 5.1 (*continued*)

Task/item	Commentary and examples
	A good way to work through this is to imagine a client 'walking' through all the areas on the site and to describe what they will see It does not have to be very detailed at this stage. An overall schema/wish list will suffice
What specific functionality do you want? (Check Chapter 2 for what's possible)	For example: • ability to up- and download documents; • online conferencing facilities – ability to share documents, get into live chat etc.; • 'push' e-mail – when a new item gets posted to automatically generate an e-mail to the client's inbox; • ability to fill in an initial instruction form; • ability to pay for documents online Again, walk the client through the process and describe what they can do/how the system will interact with them This does not have to be very detailed, an outline will suffice
Content management Where will the internal content for your site come from? Who/what will be the source?	For example: • special reports on matter progress generated by the practice management system (PMS); • word documents from client file; • financial information from accounts system; • news items from external news clipping agency
Outline a list of the types of content Do you want to use third party providers to collate and present specialist news?	For example: • news from the firm – written specifically in-house/PR agency • external news provided by news agency • information about the firm – written specifically by copywriter from web design agency • Word documents from file server/PMS • report on milestones – PMS/Case Management • report on running record of costs – PMS

Table 5.1 (*continued*)

Task/item	Commentary and examples
Who will be responsible for updating the content? How often?	Part of the specification for your new system can also include a content management system that will enable people to automatically update the website. This functionality should be included as part of your extranet design
Integration issues How do you want to integrate the website with your current systems?	Ability to merge the initial instructions form on the client extranet directly into the practice management system? Ability to automatically publish matter reports from PMS to the extranet?
Security Do you have any specific security concerns?	Your suppliers will work with you to implement the right level of security. Make sure they know about any special concerns you might have and particularly sensitive information (e.g. a high profile piece of litigation or information about a well known public figure, i.e. information that might be of more interest to hackers than the usual run-of-the-mill law firm business)

Notes

1 Webb, N. (2003) *Internet Marketing*, Law Society Publishing.
2 Chaffey, D., Mayer, R., Johnson, K. and Ellis-Chadwick, F. (2000) *Internet Marketing: Strategy, implementation and practice.* Financial Times/Prentice Hall, Harlow.
3 Bevan, N. (1999) Usability issues in website design. *Proceedings of the 6th Interactive Publishing Conference* November 1999, **www. usability.serco.com**.
4 Neilson, J. (2000) *Details in Study Methodology Can Give Misleading Results*, **www.useit.com/alertbox/990221.html**.

6

Implementing your e-business strategy and design

Having thought through how the Internet can add value to your clients and your firm, what next? How do you go from having some good ideas written down to actually making it happen?

This chapter is about implementing your e-business strategy. As with most things in the e-business world, in practice it won't be a straight linear process. One part of the process may raise issues that involve you going back to rethink an earlier part of the process. For a while it may feel like you are going round in circles and wasting valuable fee earning time. However, the process of educating yourself and your firm about what is possible through actively engaging in the implementation process is invaluable.

We will focus on the different approaches to implementing an e-business and the range and types of vendors you will need. There will be some tips on how to find vendors, how to negotiate and how to work successfully with them.

Implementation planning

> In medieval times, cathedrals were usually built without any plans. The master builder had a vague idea of a plan and began to build. As he proceeded, the builder, or his patron – a bishop, king or rich noble-man – might alter the plan. Rather than start anew the builder incorporated the changes and continued until something resembling a cathedral was complete. Usually the finished product looked nothing like the initial design.[1]

Many law firms are rather like those medieval builders and don't do project planning. There are many reasons for this, not least the fact that most key players in any project are usually also very busy fee earning and meeting time targets. As things never turn out the way you planned anyway, the temptation is to hop over this stage and just get on with it.

Stop!

So why is project planning important?

Project planning works because it tries to map out the territory you will be covering before you get there. Obviously the map isn't the territory, but the process of thinking through who will do what by when is a very good way of focusing expectations and setting realistic deadlines. Also it gives you a chance to think through the 'to do' list which often highlights areas that you haven't really considered yet.

Project planning is a professional discipline in its own right, and there are many theories and methods about how it should be done. A simple method is described below.

The project board

An important starting point is to set up a project board that is accountable for the overall delivery of the project. Board members usually consist of key stakeholders in the organisation. They take on being accountable for the project, developing the plans, finding and managing vendors and reporting back to the partnership on progress.

The project board ideally should comprise the following:

- partner;
- practice manager;
- associate fee earner;
- member of support staff.

This mix will give the range of perspectives needed to make sure what is implemented is relevant. If your project is going to be one that is particularly client focused, a brave step would be to include a client on your project board, in an advisory capacity at least, to make sure you stay on track from the client perspective.

Project planning

Clearly a plan to update your current website by adding a little extra functionality is a different order of magnitude from planning an intranet/extranet for the first time. But however small the intended change, a plan is a very good idea. There is, of course, software to help you plan the work and work the plan – Microsoft Project is probably the best known.

Project planning does not have to be a complex undertaking and even one page of A4 with well thought out key tasks will make a difference. Again, as in many of these things, the process of doing it is almost as important as the final plan.

The key things a project plan should include are described below.

Overall purpose of the project

You need to be clear about why you are doing it in the first place. For example:

> To offer excellent client care to our conveyancing clients and invite them to use our other legal services.

Objectives

These should be SMART:

- Specific
  - concrete
  - using action verbs;
- Measurable
  - numeric or descriptive
  - quantity, quality, cost;
- Attainable
  - feasible
  - appropriately limited in scope
  - within the firm's control and influence;
- Results-focused
  - measuring outputs or results (not activities)
  - including products, accomplishments;
- Timely
  - identifying target date
  - including interim steps and a plan to monitor progress.

For example:

> To have 40 per cent of our conveyancing clients use our specialist website on a regular basis (i.e. at least once a week) by September 2003.

To develop a series of fact sheets on our wills, probate and personal injury services by April 2004 that are read by 30 per cent of clients visiting our conveyancing website.

To generate x new will matters per month from our conveyancing website by May 2004.

There is no right set of objectives, just the ones that your particular firm wants to achieve. There is also no right way to draft them. The benefit is in thinking about them and writing them down.

Action plan

For each of the objectives, you need to decide who will do what task by when.

Milestones

These are key dates which represent completion of a particular set of tasks. They usually have a deliverable attached to them. The point of milestones is that they give you a snapshot of how the project is going. If you miss a date for a milestone it is likely that the project is starting to run late, whereas with some other tasks it may be acceptable for them not to be completed by a certain date as other tasks are not dependent on them. See Table 6.1 for an example.

Table 6.1 Action planning

Key task	Who is responsible	Target completion date
Develop tender document for suppliers	David (finance partner) Helen (practice manager)	15/01/04
Send out tender document	Helen	21/01/04
Review tender documents and shortlist three	David Helen Fiona (PA to senior partner)	20/02/04
Interview three on shortlist and make decision	David, Helen, Fiona	25/02/04
Milestone – vendor appointed		26/02/04

Approaches to implementing e-business infrastructure

Until very recently the common approach to implementing IT was to install a client/server network running something like Windows NT (or Novel Netware – though that's less popular these days). Most people will have a PC on their desk running standard office automation software (e.g. Microsoft Office) and some form of specialist legal software.

Traditionally law firms have developed their software in the following steps:

- word processing – originally on standalone machines and later on a network;
- accounting – again originally on a standalone machine used by the cashier and latterly on the network with fee earner access;
- time recording – sometimes with fee earners doing their own directly into the accounts system;
- case management – for those firms that have a high turnover of work in a certain area (e.g. conveyancing, personal injury, debt, etc.).

Fully integrated practice management systems that also have generic case management functionality are now very popular since they integrate all the main functions that a law firm is likely to need.

The point about all these systems though, is that they are owned and managed internally by the law firm. If something goes wrong, the vendor either dials into the server that is in the firm to try to fix it, or as a last resort sends out an engineer.

More recently some new approaches have emerged, which some firms are now experimenting with. These include:

- 'thin client' (Citrix Metaframe, Winframe) technology;
- application service provision (ASP).

Thin client

This is an arrangement where all the programs and information are held on a central server and are accessed by machines that are dumb terminals, i.e. they don't have any processing power or local hard drives to store programs and files on. All the applications are run from and the data stored on the central server with only the minimum amount of machinery on the desktop (a screen, keyboard, mouse and network connection) needed to connect to the central server. Hence the name 'thin client' – the machine on the desktop (the client) is very skinny indeed. By contrast an ordinary PC is rather fat or rich, with the capability to do the processing work on its own should the network and the server not be available.

This type of arrangement is often installed within the firm, i.e. the server is still owned and managed by the firm itself and the firm still operates a local area network (LAN) based on special cabling. The dumb terminals are connected to the LAN in the usual way.

Impact of the Internet

However, once you've got the idea of having a dumb terminal on your desktop, with all the action happening on a server, this opens up the possibility of having the central server somewhere other than in the firm. Using the Internet as the network connection (rather than a LAN based on cabling), it immediately becomes possible to operate from anywhere, using either dial-up or a fixed connection to the Internet.

This has enabled serious thinking about the next approach.

Application service provision

Some companies will now make software available on servers for rent. Quite a few of the specialist legal software vendors are now experimenting or offering this kind of service with their own software. The point is that rather than setting up your own client/server networks you can simply access all the relevant software you need over the Internet for a monthly charge. You will still need some form of infrastructure within your firm to be able to access it, but using the thin client idea, this does not have to be complex.

Application service providers have had a bit of a chequered career, with many going out of business as a result of the dot.com crash. However, some have survived and the market is now expanding again. A good place to find out about the current state of play in the general ASP market is **www.aspnews.com** where there is a directory of current ASP providers in Europe.

To ASP or not to ASP?

It is likely that there is another three-year business cycle left in the old client/server network model for two reasons. First, ASP is still in its infancy. Microsoft and the other major software vendors are still thinking through how it will all work for them. Microsoft has developed and is continuing to develop its dot Net strategy which is about web-enabling all its software. An example of this could be the ability to store Word documents directly onto a web server somewhere on the Internet in exactly the same way that you store documents on the hard disk or server at present. Secondly, the only really effective way to deliver ASP as a robust service is via an ADSL or higher bandwidth link. Given the current issues around the roll-out of ADSL across the country there is still some way to go. The message, then, is to keep the current set-up for a little longer, but to keep your ear to the ground. There are some very real benefits to the ASP model, not least being able to outsource the headache of IT infrastructure maintenance to professionals who you can hold accountable. Many specialist legal IT vendors are also on the case and it is worth a chat with your current vendor to find out the pros and cons.

Outsourcing

Large commercial companies who intend to take their e-business operations seriously have to choose between running the operation themselves in-house, that is buying and managing the web servers and making these available to the Internet, and outsourcing it to a third party vendor.

It is likely that most law firms will want and need to outsource their e-business infrastructure since they are unlikely to have the internal IT skills needed to build and manage it. In fact it is also possible to outsource internal operations. This means having an external vendor take over the procurement and running of your in-house systems, which is an option for some larger firms. How this works is that you pay a fixed monthly or annual fee to a vendor who then is responsible for providing the network and all the software that you require. The vendor is accountable for managing the infrastructure and providing maintenance and ongoing support. A lot of government departments and the Law Society currently manage their IT in this way.

However, for smaller firms this may not be an option and most opt to purchase their own in-house IT, have vendors install it and then either use the same vendors, or specialist support companies to manage it.

What types of IT vendors do you need?

To build and implement an e-business solution you will need IT vendors to supply the following components:

- internal network with Internet access, e-mail and a firewall plus additional server(s) for intranet if required;
- internal software, e.g. Microsoft Office, specialist legal software;
- website design and building;
- ISP to register and manage domain name, provide Internet e-mail and host website(s);
- integration – vendor to provide the elements needed to integrate the internal systems with the external website.

Unless you have in-house IT staff dedicated to the task, you will also need a vendor to provide ongoing maintenance and support via a help desk. It is also useful if they are able to dial in to your server(s) and manage them remotely.

It is likely that you already have someone who has provided you with the basic internal infrastructure such as the network and internal software. If you run specialist legal software you probably get maintenance and support from your vendor for their software and you may also use them to manage your network, or perhaps another third party to manage it for you. In-house IT systems are beyond the scope of this book, but you can find more information about selecting and managing legal IT at **www.opportunity-consulting.co.uk**.

One area that you will probably not want to outsource is providing the content to your site as this is a fundamental part of maintaining client relationships – knowing what to post to the site when. Having said this, there are still opportunities to outsource the production of marketing material and things like news feeds to your site (for example, **www.words4business.com**).

What IT should you already have in place?

This is a difficult question to answer and is probably more about the level of IT awareness and understanding in your firm than the actual nuts and bolts of the technology already in place. As has been said throughout this book, e-business offers the opportunity to innovate at a level that has not been available before. This may range from a gentle evolution from where you are already, to taking on a whole new limb for your current business activities. Either way, if it has been carefully thought out from the client perspective there is no reason why it shouldn't work.

Finding the right IT vendor

Now comes the million dollar question. Who are the right vendors for the job? When it comes to specialist legal IT this has probably been one of the most vexed questions facing smaller law firms – with around 50 specialist legal IT firms in the market finding the right one has been a major concern. Most law firms are now well into their second or even third generation of IT. Whatever e-business options you are deciding to implement it is likely that your specialist legal IT vendor will have a role to play, even if it's only explaining to you, or your chosen website developer, how to get information from their systems so it can be made available on the web.

The process for finding vendors

The key to a successful implementation is working with your vendor as if they were a business partner. This involves a different approach to the one you'd take if you were simply buying something off the shelf. There has to be a fit, not just of products, services and skills but also the intangibles such as 'do we get on?' A 70/30 rule applies. This means that 30 per cent is about whether they can the do the job ('do they have the know-how, skills, products and services we're looking for?') and 70 per cent is 'do we like them?', 'will they give us the ongoing quality of service and support that we deserve?'

Tendering for supply

The traditional tendering process, described below, is a useful way to find the right people for the job.

1. Select a team from within the firm to manage the tendering process.
2. Work out what you want and what's missing (most of the thinking should now have been done through the process of developing an e-business strategy and design).
3. Develop a Request for Information (RFI) document.
4. Send out the RFI to a list of vendors who appear to have what you want.
5. Receive and assess replies.
6. Develop the Invitation to Tender (ITT) document. This is a more detailed document than the RFI setting out your exact requirements and requesting more accurate costs.
7. Assess responses.
8. Make a shortlist.
9. Invite shortlist in for a meeting.
10. Assess and make decision.
11. Negotiate and sign contract for supply.

This may appear rather long-winded and bureaucratic, but it does not have to be so. The point is to aim to develop an ongoing relationship with people who are going to support you in making the most of your e-business. It is important to get it right, and although there are no guarantees, following a structured approach will help.

Establishing a team to work on the tender

This can be the project board, or a team of other people that the board nominates. The mix should be broadly similar to that of the project board, for example, a partner, associate fee earner, practice manager and support staff member. If the plan is to implement a specialist client extranet, e.g. for the conveyancing department, it makes sense to draw the team from that department.

Assessing where you are now: the IT benchmark grid

Table 6.2 shows an example of a benchmark grid with various levels. These reflect the traditional implementation of hardware and IT applications in law firms. The purpose of this is to give you some idea of a benchmark for your IT development rates in terms of basic IT infrastructure.

The general idea is that firms move towards the highest level (7). However, it may be that certain components, for example case management, are not suitable for your level of operations and/or that you are too small to implement document management or formal knowledge management systems – there is no hard and fast rule about what level you should aim for. As a general rule of thumb, e-business can be usefully contemplated around level 4, taking the evolutionary rather than revolutionary approach.

Prerequisites

The starting point is to ensure that you have some basic IT plumbing in place that is well managed, has proper maintenance and support and that most firm members are competent in using. For example:

- a network that is connected through a firewall to the Internet allowing e-mail and web browsing;
- everyone in the firm having a PC, or thin client – including fee earners;
- some form of client/matter database and document production and management (practice/case management system). This is likely to be the source of most of the information that is of interest and use to clients if you are developing a client extranet.

It is advisable that your current internal systems are as integrated as possible. Integration was discussed in Chapter 4. If you don't have this in place already, then start here before getting involved with developing further e-business capability. The old adage about building on firm foundations applies.

Table 6.2 IT benchmark grid

Level	Hardware			Internal Software							Internet			
	PCs standalone	PCs networked	Remote working	Word processing	Diary/ outlook	Accounts (view)	Time recording	PMS	Case Mgmt	Doc Mgmt/ knowledge mgmt	E-mail	Net access	Website*	Intranet
0	S			S		S								
1	A			A		A								
2		S		S	S	S								
3		A		A	A	A	S/A				S/A	S/A	1?	
4		A	S	A	A	A	A	S/A			A	A	1	
5		A	S	A	A	A	A	A			A	A	1/2	
6		A	S	A	A	A	A	A	S	S/A	A	A	2/3	
7		A	A	A	A	A	A	A	A/S	A	A	A	3/4	A

Key

Level 0 = Some support staff, e.g. cashier, have a PC running standalone accounts and secretaries have standalone word processing (WP)

Level 1 = Everyone in the firm has a standalone PC running WP with access to viewing the accounts

Level 2 = There is a limited PC network running accounts and WP and maybe MS Office – usually only the support staff have PCs

Level 3 = Everyone has a networked PC running accounts, WP, online time recording (e.g. support staff enter it) with some or all having e-mail and Internet access

Level 4 = Everyone has a networked PC running accounting, time recording, e-mail, Internet access

Level 5 = Everyone has a networked PC, with access to an integrated practice management system (including accounts and time recording, WP, e-mail and with Internet access

Level 6 = Everyone has a networked PC running an integrated practice management system. There may be a case management system for key areas of work (if appropriate) and some form of document and knowledge management system beyond that provided by WP

Level 7 = Everyone has a networked PC, with access to integrated practice management system, full range of office software, e-mail, Internet access, document and knowledge management probably over an intranet. Remote working is available to everyone

S = Some staff have this

A = All staff have this

*Website: 1 = brochureware; 2 = interactivity; 3 = e-commerce/online service; 4 = e-business (e.g. client extranet).

First steps: an intranet?

Some people also argue that a prerequisite for an effective e-business is having a fully functional intranet in place. This does offer a good starting point, since it provides not only the benefits of having your internal information resources organised effectively, which then provided food for the external websites, but also provides an excellent learning opportunity to get to grips with the technologies before venturing out onto the Internet and getting clients fully engaged.

However, some firms feel that they want to cut straight to the chase and get on with delivering added value to clients, arguing that a lot of energy could be wasted focusing internally. There is no right or wrong way and the approach is entirely up to you.

The request for information

This is usually used for two purposes: finding out which vendors have the types of products and services you require and getting ballpark figures for your business case (see Chapter 4 on e-business strategy). Another use for the process is to learn about what is available in the market enabling you to adapt your design and plans accordingly. It is important not to confuse this process with a full tender. This is more like doing some market research to help inform your planning, business case and the tender that comes later.

If your requirements are relatively simple, for example, you just want additional functionality for an existing website, you may choose to go straight to the tender stage.

An RFI should be short and to the point, outlining very briefly what you want in simple terms and asking for feedback on four key issues:

- Is what you're proposing 'doable' – or is there a better way to do it?
- Can the vendor provide the required products and services?
- If so, how much is it likely to cost? – an approximation is sufficient at this stage.
- What are the gaps? Can the vendor suggest things you've not thought about? And what are the risks?

Sending out the RFI to likely contenders

Finding a list of vendors is often a stumbling block for firms. Here are some likely information sources:

- your own specialist legal IT supplier and/or network provider;
- vendors in the Law Society's annual *Software Solutions Guide* (**www.it.lawsociety.org.uk**);
- other specialist legal IT vendors and legal publishers, find listings at:
  - **www.venables.co.uk**
  - **www.lawzone.co.uk**
  - **www.legaltechnology.com**
- specialist legal web design agencies, e.g.
  - **www.activelawyer.com**
  - **www.lawyersonline.co.uk**;
- general web design agencies (do a search using Google and surf the web), e.g.
  - **www.newmediaaid.co.uk** offers a £19 per hour service at the time of writing;
- web magazines also have many advertisements and directory listings can be found at Yahoo! and other general purpose portals.

Send out three to five RFIs to a range of potential vendors, including at least one from the non-legal world. It is often enlightening to see the different approaches that companies take and you can learn a great deal from their responses. If you already have an idea of who you would like to tender to, then by all means go straight to the tender stage. Make sure you put a 'by when' date in the RFI and make sure that companies have at least two weeks to respond. Remember to acknowledge the responses and let the companies know your timetable for tendering so that you are not pestered by salesmen.

Assessing RFI responses

Apply your normal judgement to this. As well as considering cost, use your instinct about which vendors feel right. This is not a scientific process. Look at their websites and the portfolio of sites they have been involved in. This will give you an overall impression of the style of the company.

Make a shortlist of those to whom you want to send out a full Invitation to Tender document.

Developing the Invitation to Tender document

There has been a tendency in the past to make Invitation to Tender documents very detailed indeed, particularly if you employ an external IT consultant. Vendors dislike complex ITTs, not because they are trying to hide anything, but because they take time and money to prepare, and often don't provide answers to the real questions that people want to ask. This is much better done in a meeting, which is what you will eventually be basing your decision on anyway.

Keep the ITT document brief and to the point, but do share what your business vision is and how you hope your e-business will support and enhance this. Vendors say that this really helps them to focus their responses in a way that will be genuinely helpful to you. Also include some background information on your firm and the findings from your IT assessment. This also helps vendors get a feel for you and target their responses accordingly. By revealing this kind of information about yourself you give vendors the opportunity to try to be a fit with your firm. How well they manage to do this will be a key indicator for deciding whether you want to work with them.

Contents for the ITT should include:

- a brief outline of the firm;
- your business vision;
- what you want to achieve with e-business;
- how you are thinking about going about it (see your e-business strategy and design);
- your current IT set-up;
- what you want from the vendor:
    - brief details about their company,
    - what they intend to supply and how they intend to supply it,
    - how this will deliver your e-business vision,
    - costs,
    - project management capability,
    - a list of other clients,

- any other information they think will be helpful, e.g. the strategic vision they have for their own firm,
- evidence of financial stability,
- CVs of staff to work on the project (if relevant);
- an outline of your timescales and when you want the whole thing implemented by;
- the closing date;
- firm contact details (a named person to respond to queries about the tender).

Send this out to the shortlist you developed from the RFI – three is a good rule of thumb.

Assessing ITT responses

Clearly, the quality of the answers is dependent on the quality of the questions. However, again common sense applies. Look beyond cost to see if there is a strategic fit between you and the vendor and for evidence of whether you like them.

Key things to look out for include:

- Have they answered the questions you asked, or does the document have the feel of being a standard response?
- Have they given some thought to what you want, or are they proposing a stock solution?
- Have they covered how they will help you implement the system, the type of people they will make available to you, and how long implementation is likely to take?
- Have they demonstrated a real understanding of legal business?
- What is the ratio of development/sales and marketing/ support and help desk staff? There is some anecdotal evidence that shows companies that have larger support teams tend to be more customer oriented.

Meetings

This is where you will get a real opportunity to assess who you would like to work with. Use structured interviewing techniques – have a list of preset questions that you ask all vendors. The kinds of questions you ask can range around the ones outlined above for assessing the tender document. Allow some time for free-ranging discussion. It is likely that vendors will also want to demonstrate their wares in some form and make sure that you have discussed their technical requirements with them.

Limit the interview to a maximum of two hours per vendor.

Assessing and making your decision

Having met with your shortlist it's now time to make a decision. There is no easy way to do this as it will be based on a range of hard and soft factors and people will have different opinions. It is important at this stage to ensure that you understand everything that is on offer and that there are no hidden costs.

The vendor should also have supplied some customer references. Take time to call these and ask some questions including:

- What do you think are their strengths and weaknesses?
- Have you had any issues around ongoing support with them?
- Would you recommend them?

Be sure to write down the responses and discuss them with a range of colleagues before coming to a final conclusion. A useful safety check is to invite the front-runner in to give another presentation/demonstration to a larger group from the firm before making the final decision.

Negotiating the contract for supply

This can be one of the hardest parts of the process since this is where you agree on exactly what will be supplied by when. If you are not sure of anything you should check before you sign the contract. It is amazing how many law firms simply sign a standard contract for supply without reading it, only to find that when their expectations are not met, they were not part of the original contract.

Things to make sure you cover include:

- Roles and responsibilities, exactly who will be responsible for doing what by when?
- What are the agreed timescales – are there any penalties (on both sides) for not making agreed deadlines?
- What are the agreed costs? Are there any extra costs for on-going maintenance and support? What will these be after year 1?

- What functionality must be included in the system? Are there special requirements, e.g.
  - Who is responsible for managing the ISP/hosting of the website? Are they to use your current ISP or will they find and manage one for you?
- If you spend time designing a bespoke system together, make sure you own the intellectual property.
- What are you going to do in the case of dispute – seek mediation first?

However, while seeking to be sensible about this, don't get too carried away. The point is to get a good e-business system up and running, not to have the most perfect 300-page contract for supply.

Working with vendors

You will now work with your chosen vendors to set about implementing the system you have designed. Mission critical is making sure that you have a project manager in place who will oversee the whole project. Each vendor will have their own approach to how they like to plan the work to be done. You should have already planned out how you want the project to go. Working in conjunction with the vendor to revise and amend the plan is a very good idea before you sign the contract for supply.

Understanding the role of project management in implementation

One of the main problems preventing law firms from really engaging with technology, and in particular e-business, is that for legal professionals, the whole process of buying and implementing technology seems incredibly complex and difficult. In speaking to law firms over the years, one of the key components that appears to be missing is understanding the concept of project management. This is not just about the process of getting things done, but the wider concept of planning a project, identifying all the resources – both internal and external – that are needed to make it happen, and then managing those resources to deliver the intended outcomes.

In theory this sounds relatively simple, but in practice managing the boundary between in-house and out of house causes
extreme difficulty. This boils down to the simple questions, 'who
owns the project?' and 'who is accountable for implementing it?'

On the surface the answers are also simple: 'we (the firm)
own the project' and 'they (the vendor) are accountable for
implementing it'. However, where problems and breakdowns
occur is that the vendor does not own the internal resources
(people and information) that are often needed to implement the
project effectively. They are not at liberty to direct people's time
and energy to making things happen internally. Yet this is fundamentally important since the success of the implementation
project will always depend on people in your firm doing things
that are outside their normal routine tasks. This can range from
providing the information needed to customise software to fit the
way you work (in the case of practice/case management systems)
to providing people to do tasks that are part of implementing the
system, for example formatting documents.

Training is a fundamental issue. This does not just mean
being available to be trained, but actually listening and learning
something in the training session believing that it's important.
Engaging fully in training is possibly the most important
implementation issue.

As part of the tendering process you have to be clear exactly
what services you are looking for. If you don't have a dedicated
in-house project manager then you will need to have this service
as part of your implementation plan. There will always be a ten-
sion if you elect to have the vendor responsible for the project
management, since they are commercial organisations looking to
do things as quickly and cheaply as possible.

Managing website development

Built into your project plan should be the opportunity to review
and assess the designs that your website developers come up with.
They should provide you with a development area online where
you can see the site being developed before it goes live where you
can comment on it.

Review the section in Chapter 5 on what makes good web
design and ensure that this is incorporated. Design – look and
feel – is a very personal thing and it's often difficult to get every-

one to agree on what looks the best. Bear in mind that the site is meant to appeal to your target audience of clients. You are not looking for the supercool website award. The acid test is whether the site is practical and easy to use. This will far outweigh how slick it looks.

Changing working practices

This is an area that also causes headaches when it comes to implementing new IT effectively. For e-business it is even more important to manage the transition from the way you currently work to the new way of working. This is the greatest source of breakdown for law firms and is often forgotten in the rush to get the new system in. In particular, working practices that involve both a manual and IT element cause the most difficulty. Staff, who have become used to working in one particular way, are now asked to work in a different way.

The starting point is to prepare a detailed analysis of what processes are going to change, how they are going to change and how they are going to be implemented. This is the kind of task that a vendor, with the best will in the world, cannot really help you with. They can share with you the benefit of their expertise in implementing systems in other organisations, but it is down to you to make it work in your firm.

Approaches to implementation

Depending on the size of the project you are planning to implement there are various approaches:

- the big bang;
- phasing;
- piloting;
- prototyping.

The big bang

This is essentially where you implement everything at once. This may be an appropriate approach depending on what it is you want to do. For example, if you are going to put your conveyancing department online, there may not be an easy way to split this into discrete parts to phase in implementation.

Overall this is the highest risk approach.

Phasing

This is where you split the implementation into bite size chunks and implement one phase at a time. You ensure that each stage is up and running before you go on to the next phase. This is a low to medium risk strategy. The problem can be that your implementation becomes perpetual as you keep adjusting what you are doing and never reach a conclusion. This is a recipe for having costs run out of control.

Piloting

This entails implementing the whole system for a limited number of clients/staff. This is a particularly good approach when you are not sure whether what you have designed is going to make the difference you anticipate. You can also pilot a small subset of what you intend to see how it goes.

This is a low risk strategy since it gives you the opportunity to adjust your overall plan as you go along. However, it too needs managing closely as there is the opportunity for costs to go out of control as both clients and staff request more and more changes to the design. It works to 'freeze' the requirements at a given stage and get them up and working.

Prototyping

Prototypes are initial versions of a website that have the basic features and structure of the solution but without all the content and services in place. The prototype is then used to test the concept with potential users to gain feedback. There are three sorts of prototype:

- *Throwaway prototype* – this is not kept as a basis for the final system and is sometimes paper based or developed in tools such as Microsoft Powerpoint.
- *Evolutionary prototype* – this is not discarded, but acts as the basis for the next iteration of the system.
- *Incremental prototype* – this can be combined with evolution-

ary prototyping. It is where modules of the system are proto-
typed until each is complete, and eventually the whole system
becomes complete.

Prototyping means that you get to iron out potential flaws in the
thinking and design of the website before going live.

Policies and procedures

Part of your implementation process should be the development
of the following policies:

- privacy and client confidentiality – the promises you make
  about how you are going to use client data that is collected
  online;
- disclaimers;
- how you intend to get opt-in permission for sending e-mails.

Which? Online has started a Web Trader scheme which has a com-
prehensive code of practice for trading online (**http://webtrader.
which.net**).

Data Protection Act 1998

Check **www.dataprotection.gov.uk** to find out the latest information on this. Here is a summary of what firms must do:

1. Inform the user, before asking for information, on:
    (a) who the firm is;
    (b) what personal data is collected and stored;
    (c) the purpose of the collection.
2. Ask for consent for collecting personal sensitive data; it is
    good practice to ask before collecting any kind of data.
3. Provide a statement of a privacy policy. 'A privacy statement
    helps individuals to decide whether or not to visit the site,
    and when they do visit, whether or not to provide any
    personal information to the data controller.'
4. Always let individuals know when cookies or other covert
    software is being used to collect information about them.
5. Never collect or retain personal data unless it is strictly necess-
    ary for the organisation's purposes. For example, a person's

name and address should not be required to provide an online quotation. If extra information is required for marketing purposes this should be made clear and the provision of such information should be optional.

6. Amend incorrect data when informed and tell others. Enable correction onsite.
7. Only use data for marketing (by the company, or third parties) when a user has been informed that this is the case and has agreed to this (opt in).
8. Provide the option for customers to stop receiving information (opt out).
9. Use technology to protect the customer information on your site.

Ongoing management of the website

Once they have their website up and running, many firms heave a huge sigh of relief and promptly forget all about it. While this is not fatal for a brochureware site, it is mortal death for an e-business website be it an intranet, extranet or public website with client facing functionality.

There are many approaches to managing a website, but the best ones are based on seeing it as part of the client care and marketing process, as opposed to managing it as an IT system. Some firms have developed a web committee that functions rather like the editorial panel for a magazine, where as much emphasis is given to content as to the physical layout and design.

This committee is responsible for developing website standards and making sure they are maintained. It should also monitor feedback from site users and specify ongoing site structure and design changes. It can also be accountable for managing external maintenance and support contracts with website developers and ISPs, as well as working with those responsible for the overall IT infrastructure of the firm. The committee should be client (marketing) and content focused rather than technically focused.

The group should also keep their collective eye on the usage of the site (see section on metrics in Chapter 7 on e-marketing) and make adjustments to the site accordingly.

Content management

As has been stressed throughout this book, fresh content is the food that keeps a good website alive. With this in mind it is important to make sure that content management processes are part of the overall design and implementation of the new system.

Day-to-day updating

There are two aspects to this:

- Who will be responsible for the various aspects of content management – who will produce the content, who will check it and who will authorise it before it is published online?
- How do you want the system to work to do this – how integrated and automated does it need to be?

In the past, content used to be 'hardwired' to the HTML pages and to change it required knowledge of HTML programming. These days various systems are available to enable ordinary users to post content to sites. More sophisticated versions also enable the routing of content around the firm so that it can be signed off by a senior person responsible before being published to the website.

The frequency of updates is a major issue that will need to be determined based on the nature and usage of the website.

Working with Internet Service Providers

It is likely that your web developers and/or specialist legal software suppliers will manage this aspect of things for you. However, if you are planning a small project it may be helpful to know something about managing ISPs.

The primary issue in managing ISPs is to ensure satisfactory service quality at a reasonable price. Issues include:

- speed of access
  - speed of server
  - bandwidth;
- availability;
- service level agreements;
- security.

Speed of access refers to the speed at which the end user can download pages from your website (i.e. have them appear in their browser, *not* downloaded and stored on their hard disk). It is governed by two factors: the speed of the server on which the website is hosted and the speed of the connection of the web server to the Internet. The fastest site will be running on a web server dedicated to your site, with large amounts of memory (RAM) and with a fast connection (large bandwidth) to the Internet. See Chapter 2 for a technical explanation of these terms.

Availability refers to the amount of time the server is available for access on the Internet. Obviously it should be available as close to 100 per cent as possible, but for various reasons sometimes this is not the case.

Service level agreements – to ensure the best speed and availability you should check the service level agreements carefully. The agreements will define confirmed standards of availability and performance measured in terms of the latency or network delay when information is passed from one point to another.

Security. This is a very important topic (see Chapter 2 for further discussion on this). Check what the security arrangements are for your ISP. For example, you may opt to have a dedicated web server for your site that has its own firewall between it and the ISP's network. The ISP will also have a series of security features between its own servers and the Internet including firewalls too.

Which are the best ISPs?

Several UK Internet magazines – such as *Internet Works* (**www.iwks.com**) and *Internet Magazine* (**www.internet-magazine.com**) – provide monthly performance assessments of different ISPs.

Services for companies to assess their performance are also provided by Keynote (**www.keynote.com**), Zeus (**www.zeus.co.uk**) and (**www.webperf.net**) and Mercury Interactive (**www.mercuryinteractive.com**).

Note

1   Kalakolta, R. and Robinson, M. (2001) *E-business 2.0*, Addison-Wesley.

7

E-marketing

The subject of e-marketing, like its offline counterpart, is a large topic indeed, embracing as it does everything to do with clients and the range and type of legal services you offer them. In many ways marketing is the context within which you should consider the whole area of e-business, since it defines the whole purpose and nature of a business. When most law firms think about marketing, they really mean advertising and promoting the firm, but promotion is only a small subset of the marketing discipline.

This chapter will examine online activity as a means of building client loyalty and long-term relationships with existing clients. The focus is deliberately on technology rather than marketing techniques as there are many other books on the specific topic of e-marketing (see *Internet Marketing*, edited by Nicola Webb, published by the Law Society, 2003).

Relationship marketing

Marketing is all about relationships. Relationships with clients, lapsed clients and potential clients. The firm also has relationships with suppliers, for example counsel, staff and other stakeholders, like the Legal Services Commission, but this discussion will look at client relationship marketing.

Relationship marketing shifts the focus away from one-off transaction marketing towards developing a longer-lasting relationship with your client that ideally develops into a lifetime relationship.

Permission marketing

Building relationships is a delicate affair. They progress through three stages, beginning with permission then trust and ultimately loyalty. Much of relationship building is common sense, but often in the race to get the legal work done effectively the relationship side of things can be ignored.

Godin (1999)[1] outlines several steps towards permission marketing:

1. *Gaining permission*. The first step is to get the client's permission to give them information over and above what they think they are paying you for. In many ways solicitors are lucky in that they are a trusted source of information and gaining permission is relatively easy, provided clients don't think it's another ruse to add billable time.
2. *Collaboration*. Marketing is a collaborative activity where marketers help clients buy and clients help marketers sell. In the legal world focused marketing activity that helps a client avoid legal risk – being the fence at the top of the cliff rather than the ambulance at the bottom – is a good value proposition. In return clients can give feedback on what works best for them, but only if they are asked.
3. *Dialogue*. A dialogue emerges whether via website e-mails, discussion rooms, real conversations in focus groups or even real meetings between customers and sales reps. Dialogue involves both speaking and listening. In the legal world, firms need to listen to what clients are saying, and sometimes this isn't a verbal exchange. For example, in a conveyancing practice, how many of your clients return for a second transaction, be it a re-mortgage, a will or some other legal service? In a pile 'em high, sell 'em cheap world the dialogue element can be overlooked.

Permission marketing involves developing the relationship and winning permission to talk on a regular basis. There is a tendency in law firms to consider the client as finished with once the matter is completed. What would it take to continue the interaction after a matter closes? Some law firms have been very astute at this by getting permission to provide legal information directly to a commercial client's intranet on an ongoing basis. In the private client world, the traditional method of staying in touch has been to store the client's will and deeds which have been seen as a reason to contact the client from time to time. However, very few firms take a proactive approach to this, mainly because they haven't been upfront at the outset about wanting to stay in touch. Taking a proactive approach by gaining permission at the beginning of the relationship opens up new possibilities for relationship building.

Choosing clients

Of course, you can choose the range and type of client with whom you want this kind of relationship. You don't have to do it with all clients and in fact with some there may be little point. But following the 80/20 rule where it's likely that 80 per cent of your income comes from 20 per cent of your clients, it makes sense to nurture the 20 per cent.

In the legal business context there will be some clients who just want a quick and cost effective fix, whilst there will be others, for example long-term commercial clients, for whom building a long-term relationship can bring serious added value to both sides. The long-term relationship is imperative in dealing with bulk referrers as well.

Client relationship management

Approaching relationship marketing from a slightly different angle, the concept of client relationship management (CRM) has become a new buzz term over the past few years. The Internet provides a phenomenal opportunity to grow new business because of the (truly global) reach it provides.

However, it has also empowered customers and clients to shop around and find new and better deals far more easily than was possible in the offline world. Businesses can no longer count on the inertia of customers buying from the same providers because it's too much hassle to find someone else. As traditional high street firms know, having a shop front next to the estate agents is no longer the advantage it once was.

In this context, building client loyalty by focusing on building a long-term client relationship has risen to the forefront, together with a whole set of web enabled tools and techniques.

There are three phases to client relationship management, which are illustrated in Figure 7.1. They are:

- *client acquisition* which involves techniques to form relationships with new clients;
- *client retention* which refers to the actions a firm takes to retain existing clients;

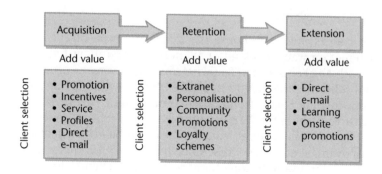

Figure 7.1 The three phases of client relationship management
© Chaffey, D. (2002) *E-Business and E-Commerce Management,* Pearson Education Limited.
Reprinted by permission of Pearson Education Limited.

- *client extension* which refers to increasing the depth or range of services bought from the firm.

At each stage there is also *client selection* where you choose the types of client with whom you want to interact, for example a commercial client who requires ongoing legal services.

Client acquisition management

In an online context, client acquisition can have two meanings:

- using a website to acquire new clients;
- encouraging existing clients into an online dialogue.

The focus for law firms tends to be on the latter. As has been pointed out elsewhere in this book, firms have not had a great deal of success in attracting new clients directly through their websites. However, this is not to say that it is impossible and this section looks at the four main methods of online marketing communications:

- search engine registration;
- link building;
- viral marketing;
- banner advertising.

Search engine registration

Try this as an experiment. Go to a well known search engine, for example **www.google.com** and type in 'law firms in the UK' and see who turns up at the top of the list. See if your firm's website appears anywhere within the top 10 or 20. What you will notice is that the law firm directories feature prominently at the top of the list. Now try typing in your location, for example 'law firms in Torquay'. As you will quickly discover, search engines may not be the best way to get noticed.

However, that doesn't mean you can ignore them since search engines and directories are the primary method of finding information about a firm and its services. Over 80 per cent of web users say that they use search engines to find information. It follows that if your site is not listed in a search engine then people won't find it through this method.

There are many well known search engines each employing slightly different methods to index web pages. For a review of current techniques refer to **www.searchenginewatch.com** which has a full list of search engines together with tips for getting listed.

How search engines work

There are five main parameters on which search engines base the order of their ranking. These chiefly rely on how well the keywords typed in by the searcher match the same words on the page of your website. The parameters are summarised in Table 7.1 in approximate order of importance.

Getting listed

You can also submit your website to search engines, rather than relying on them to find you via their automated robots and spiders. There are a number of companies on the web that offer this service at very reasonable prices (**www.submitit.co.uk**).

Link building

A site's traffic will clearly increase with a greater number of links into it. Efforts to increase the number of links are sometimes referred to as link building. Ways of building links include:

Table 7.1 Search engine parameters

Factor	Description	Interpretation
Title	The keywords in the title of a web page that appear at the top of the browser window are indicated in the HTML code by the <TITLE>keyword</TITLE> tag	This is more likely to be listed highly if it matches the search words
Meta tags	These keywords are part of a web page, hidden from users, but used by search engines with 'robots' or 'spiders' to compile their indexes. There are two types of meta tag. Example: <meta name = 'keywords' content = 'law, lawyer, free, legal, advice'> <meta name = 'description' content = 'Probably the best law firm in the world'>	In most search engines, if a keyword is typed in that matches the words in the meta tags then this will be listed higher than sites that don't use meta tags
Frequency of occurrence	The number of occurrences of the keyword in the text of the web page will also determine the listing. Higher listings will also occur if the keyword is near the top of the page	Copy can be written to increase the number of times a word is used and boost the position in the search engine
Hidden graphic text	For example, text about a firm's name and services can be assigned to the firm's logo using the ALT tag as follows: <IMG NAME = Ourlogo' SRC='logo.gif ALT= The law firm for conveyancing'>	A site that uses a lot of graphic material is less likely to be listed highly, but it is essential that the hidden graphic text keyword is used
Links	Some search engines rank more highly when keywords entered are included as links. Others such as Google rank you more highly when there are links in from other sites	A link building campaign can help increase your position in search engines

- *Reciprocal links*. These are two-way links agreed between two organisations. A web ring is a similar arrangement between more than two organisations.
- *PR* – content mentions. This is where links to your site are included in things like online newsletters ('e-zines') and offline newspapers and trade magazines.
- *Affiliates*. Affiliate networks are widely used by e-tailers to drive traffic to their sites. They pay commission on sales referred from other sites. Amazon has in excess of 500,000 affiliates which have links to the Amazon site. Building affiliate networks is often outsourced to specialists such as **www.ukaffiliates.com**.
- *Sponsorship*. Paid for sponsorship of another site or part of it, especially a portal for an extended period is another way to develop permanent links.
- *Banner advertising*. This is a technique widely used by B2C companies to drive traffic to their sites and is described in more detail below.

Viral marketing

Viral marketing harnesses the network effect of the Internet and can be effective in reaching a large number of people around the world in the same way that a computer virus can spread (hence the name). A simple method is the 'e-mail a friend' button on a page where the page can be forwarded via e-mail to a colleague.

Banner advertising

Banner ads appear on a site and the user clicks through them to the advertiser's site. Banner ads are one of the main revenue models for the Internet so there is a lot of research undertaken into how to make them effective.

Payment is typically according to the number of customers who view the page as a cost per thousand and is usually in the range £10 to £50. How the number of customers, or traffic to the website, is measured is described later on in the chapter.

Although the death of banner ads has been predicted since they were first introduced, the value of global banner advertising has increased year on year. By 1999 it had reached $3.3 billion or 1 per cent of total global advertising revenue and Forrester

Research has predicted it could reach 10 per cent within five years.

The main argument for the decline of banner ads is that while they currently have a novelty value – a million new users join the Internet every month and may click on banner ads out of curiosity or ignorance – more experienced users tend to ignore them. Data at eMarketer (**www.emarketer.com**) shows a dramatic decline in the average click-through rate over time.

Integration with offline marketing communications

Integration of online communication with offline communication is the most effective way of ensuring traffic to a website. This means making sure that the site address is printed on all stationery, and appears in all print-based advertising. The offline techniques that are most effective include print, television, radio, PR and word of mouth.

Clearly, if you have developed a client extranet, a very important part of this will be letting your clients know about it with instructions on how to use it. This could be part of your client care procedures, including a simple printed instruction sheet that is also mirrored in an e-mail. Naturally this should promote the firm's brand.

The overall message is that your website should be included in your general marketing plan as another distribution method as well as a service in its own right.

Client retention management

Client retention has two distinct goals:

- to retain clients;
- to keep clients using the online channel – your website/client extranet.

Ideally marketing communications should address both aims. Maintaining online client relationships is difficult, and it is important to analyse the drivers of satisfaction, since satisfaction drives loyalty which drives profitability.

Building client loyalty

Statistics say that retaining existing customers is five times more profitable than acquiring new ones. In terms of commercial clients this is certainly true, particularly those who have ongoing legal service needs. For smaller high street firms the point is that at the very least, cross-selling is likely to be easier and therefore more profitable than going out and finding new clients.

All marketers know that building long-term relationships with the ideal client is essential for any sustainable business. We want to move clients up what Considine and May (1981)[2] called the 'ladder of loyalty'; see Figure 7.2.

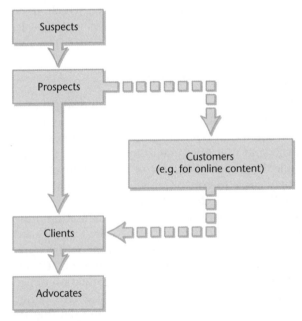

Figure 7.2 Ladder of loyalty

Some clients are likely to be more loyal than others. Firms need to focus on these rather than those who are 'promiscuous' and will hop from firm to firm looking for the cheapest deal. Clients also tend to be loyal towards a particular fee earner rather than the firm. The ideal situation for most law firms is that their clients become loyal lifetime clients – as in the old days when solicitors might be considered family friends. So how do you develop loyalty and strong relationships with clients?

- *Quality legal service, quality client care and quality sites* are pre-requisites. In fact satisfying clients should be replaced by delighting clients as research shows that even satisfied clients will often defect.
- *Privacy and security* – clients have always been able to count on solicitors keeping their affairs confidential. This should be reinforced online.
- *Integrate your service with their systems.* Some larger firms now provide legal content directly onto their commercial clients' intranets and are prepared to answer simple e-mails as part of this service.
- *Reward your clients for doing business online with you.* There are many ways of doing this, most of which don't involve money, for example providing them with free legal news-letters and updates.

How do you generate client delight?

First, by giving unexpected extra service and added value. Start by thinking about what needs your clients have and then see how you can add value. The difficult part is finding time to think about this and then the time to implement it. Sometimes it can be simple things like offering to visit an elderly client rather than have them come to you, or remembering to make an after-hours call to talk at a time that suits the client.

Secondly, by personalisation. Personalisation and mass cus-tomisation can have a high value. They can be used to tailor information on both the website and opt-in e-mail. Client extranets are a way to deliver personalisation. Other examples include developing a range of client information bulletins which are more tailored to individual types of clients rather than the traditional printed global client newsletter. Putting this kind of material together is much simpler online.

Depending on the type and range of your clients, community creation may be another appropriate way to keep them visiting your website. You may want to set up the online equivalent of a law centre, or create a community around an area of law in which you have distinct expertise, for example family law, where you take care to consider the other information needs of people who are going through divorces, child care proceedings, mediation and financial settlements.

You might like to think about what comprises loyalty drivers for your firm and brainstorm this within the firm. Ask your currently loyal clients what has them keep coming back to you.

Managing the dialogue

Too much contact can wear out the relationship. The key to building the best relationship is to have the right type and number of contacts at the right time for that specific client. Relationships are also two-way conversations. Give clients the chance to talk to you, and let them know how what they have told you has changed things, as this is a very important part of building a relationship. As it says in the 'Cluetrain Manifesto',[3] a challenging polemic on how the digital markets act as conversations.

Personalisation and mass customisation

As we saw above, personalisation and mass customisation can be used to tailor information and opt-in e-mail can be used to deliver it to add value and at the same time remind clients about what you are doing for them. Personalisation and mass customisation are terms that are often used interchangeably. In a strict sense, personalisation refers to customisation of information requested by a site client at an *individual* level. Mass customisation involves providing tailored content to a *group* with similar interests.

All these techniques make use of the dynamic possibilities provided by active server page technologies (see Chapter 5) based on a database. Preferences are stored in the database and content is taken from it. Personalisation can be achieved through several variables including:

- the client's preferences;
- the client's matter type;
- the date or time;
- particular events (e.g. certain milestones in a matter).

It can be used to offer innovative services. A good example of this is provided by online bookseller BOL (**www.bol.com**). Customers can choose their favourite parts from different types of travel guides, for example maps from the Lonely Planet guides and accommodation lists from the Rough Guides, without reference to clubs and restaurants, say. The customised book can then be printed on demand on the customer's printer.

Personalisation is much more expensive than static web pages. It requires database development and specialised software tools such as Broadvision or Bladerunner, or a bespoke application which enables users to select the content they want, recognises users when they return and displays relevant information from the database.

Extranets

Client extranets are a powerful tool, as we have seen elsewhere in this book. Since they require a unique log-in ID they enable instant personalisation. Clients can be given the option to change both the look and feel of what they see as well as the content they receive.

Opt-in e-mail ('push')

As we saw in Chapter 5, 'push' is an online communication tool which enables a targeted message to be sent to clients giving them information and at the same time reminding them about your firm and its services. They are certain to view the e-mail in their inbox, if only to delete it. Contrast this with the web, a 'pull' medium where clients have to make the decision and take action to visit your site. There is a problem, however, in that many Internet users view this type of e-mail as spam – the electronic equivalent of junk mail that appears to be even more intrusive since it arrives in personal inboxes.

Opt-in is the key to successful e-mail marketing. Client choice is the watchword. Before starting an e-mail dialogue with clients, firms must ask them to provide their e-mail address and then give them the option of opting into further communication. Ideally they should proactively opt in by checking a box. This is known as permission marketing (see above). It is likely that your client will have provided their e-mail address as part of their contact details at the outset of the matter. However, permission will be needed to use this beyond the immediate concerns of the matter. Do not assume that clients will be happy with you sending information to them that is not directly related to their matter.

Once you have collected e-mail addresses you need to plan the frequency of e-mail communication. Some options include:

- a regular newsletter – consider once a day, once a week or once a month;
- event-related – these messages would tend to be less regular, with a higher impact. It is likely that this kind of e-mail would relate to matter progress updates, etc.;
- e-mail sequence (multi-step) – some practice and case management systems now have this pre-programmed e-mail facility built in.

Designing your e-mail effectively

Designing e-mail copy is as involved as designing direct mail and many similar principles apply. Effective e-mail should:

- grab attention in the subject line and body;
- be brief – be relevant to target clients;
- be personalised, not Dear Valued Client, but Dear Mrs Brown;
- provide an opt-out or unsubscribe option by law;
- hyperlink to the website for more detailed content;
- have a clear call to action (be clear what you are asking the client to do as a result of reading the e-mail – this may well be simply to click through to your client extranet);
- be tested for effectiveness and response (try it out on guinea pigs first before doing a mass mailing);
- operate within legal and ethical constraints (including the Solicitors Publicity Code 1990).

Very good examples of this approach are the newswires sent out by LawZone (**www.lawzone.co.uk**) and the Legal Technology Insider (**www.legaltechnology.co.uk**).

Table 7.2 provides a summary of the factors required for online service quality.

Client extension

Client extension has the aim of making clients into lifelong advocates of the firm and cross-selling services to them, not just

Table 7.2 Online service quality – best practice

E-mail response requirements	Website requirements
Defined response times and named individuals responsible for replies	Support for client-preferred channel of communication in response to enquiries (e.g. choice of phone, fax, e-mail, letter or in person)
Use of autoresponders to confirm a query is being processed	Clearly indicated contact points for enquiries via e-mail and forms
Personalised e-mail where appropriate	Firm has internal targets for site availability and performance
Accurate response to inbound e-mail by client's preferred channel: outbound e-mail or phone call-back	Testing of site usability and efficiency of links, HTML, plug-ins and browsers to maximise availability
Opt-in and opt-out options must be provided for promotional e-mail with a suitable offer in exchange for clients providing details	Appropriate graphic and structural site design to achieve ease of use and relevant content with visual appeal
Clear layout, named individual and privacy statements in e-mail	Personalisation option for clients Specific tools to answer specific queries such as interactive support databases and frequently asked questions
	Compliance with Disability Discrimination Act by 2004

legal services, but other appropriate and timely services such as financial planning advice.

Direct e-mail is an excellent way for informing clients about other services that you or other allied service providers can offer, for example an independent financial advisor. You can choose which clients you want to make additional services available to and you may decide to offer them only to certain segments of your clients – those that will see them as added value rather than another sales pitch.

Another way to develop client extension is to engage clients in a dialogue about evaluating and giving feedback on your services. Properly designed (and listened to) this can provide clients with a feeling of favoured status, as everyone likes to be asked their opinion.

E-marketing measurement

Having made an investment in your website how do you know if it is achieving the desired effect? Obviously there needs to be some kind of measurement of performance.

Measurement process

A good starting point for this is to develop a measurement process which is repeatable and which relates to your overall marketing strategy and plan. An integrated measurement framework is required, otherwise you might end up just looking at things like the number of hits on the site without really finding out whether clients are happy with their experience.

A useful framework will ask the following questions:

* What do we want to achieve? This of course will be linked to your overall e-business strategy and objectives – the reasons why you are doing this in the first place.
* What is happening?
* Why is it happening?
* What should we do about it?

Collecting site visitor activity data

This records the number of visitors to the site and the paths or click-streams they take through the site as they visit different content.

Traditionally this information has been collected using log file analysis. The server-based log file is added to every time a user downloads a piece of information (a *hit*) and is analysed using a log file analyser. This is a separate program that is used to summarise the information on the client activity log file. This kind of service is usually provided by your ISP as part of their hosting fee.

Hits are not useful measures of website effectiveness since if a page consists of 10 graphics plus text it will be recorded as 11 hits. Page impressions and site visits are much better measures of site activity. A page impression denotes one person viewing one page.

Other information that packages such as Webtrends (**www.webtrends.com**) can provide through analysis of the log file includes:

- page impressions;
- entry and exit pages;
- path and click-stream analysis;
- user (visitor) sessions;
- unique users (visitors) – the number of unique visitors to a website within a set period;
- visitor frequency report (repeat visitors);
- session duration or the length of time a visitor spends on the site (a session ends after inactivity for a time set in the analyser preferences, e.g. 30 minutes) and page duration;
- country of origin;
- browser and operating system used;
- referring URL and domain (where the visitor came from).

There are, however, some issues with under- and over-counting. These are listed in Table 7.3

Table 7.3 Issues with log file analysis

Sources of under-counting	Sources of over-counting
Caching in user's web browser (when a user accesses a previously accessed file, it is loaded from the cache on the user's own PC)	Frames. A user viewing a framed page with three frames will be recorded as three page impressions on a server based system
Caching on proxy servers (proxy servers are used within organisations or by ISPs to store copies of frequently used pages and so reduce the traffic to the main site)	Spiders and robots. Traversing of a site by spiders from different search engines are recorded as page impressions. They can be excluded, but this is time consuming
Firewalls (these do not usually exclude page impressions, but they usually assign a single IP address for the user of the page, rather than each individual's PC on the network)	Executable files can also be recorded as hits or page impressions unless excluded
Dynamically generated pages, generated on the fly, are difficult to assess with server-based log files. This is likely to include any client extranet that you build	

Browser-based counting

A relatively new approach to the problem of under- and over-counting has been developed. This involves inserting a piece of Java code into each web page which interacts with the web browser and counts when a page has been downloaded into the browser. This information is then sent to a remote server. This is a more accurate way of measuring usage as it counts every time a web page is viewed by the user (see **www.redsheriff.com**).

Collecting site outcome data

Site outcome data is generated when a user performs a significant action. This is usually a transaction that is recorded, such as:

- registration to the site or subscription to an e-mail newsletter;
- request for further information such as a brochure or a request for a call back;
- responding to an online event (e.g. a web seminar);
- a sale influenced by a visit to the site;
- a sale onsite.

These activities will need to be written back to a database somewhere, either the practice/case management system and/or the database that underpins the client extranet (which may not be the same). This information will have to be integrated with the site activity information.

Summary

You need to think closely about developing your own measures and assessment frameworks that work for your firm. The point is to have at least one or two that you think will help you keep track of what is going on. Otherwise you will not know whether, in fact, your e-business activity is worthwhile and worth further investment. One of the key rules of e-business is not to be afraid of changing tack or indeed ceasing some elements of it altogether if they are not delivering the expected benefits.

Notes

1   Godin, S. (1999) *Permission Based Marketing*, Simon and Schuster, New York.

2   Considine, R. and Murray, R. (1980) *The Great Brain Robbery*, Rosebud Books, CA.

3   Levine, R. et al. (2000) *The Cluetrain Manifesto*, Pearson.

8

Change management – the liveware

> Now *here* you see, it takes all the running *you* can do, to keep in the same place. If you want to get somewhere else, you must run at least as twice as fast as that!
>
> Lewis Carroll, *Through the Looking-Glass*

I was once in a meeting with an IT vendor who said that in his experience it was rarely the hardware or the software that caused problems – it was usually the liveware. It took me a couple of seconds to realise what he was talking about – a joke similar to the one that legal practice would be great if it wasn't for the clients.

This chapter is about managing the people aspects of the change to e-business. Managing change effectively is one of the great challenges of management, and something that needs to be carefully thought out.

Key factors in achieving change

The main change levers are those major adjustments that are required in order for a firm to be agile enough to respond to changes in the marketplace and deliver competitive client service.

They are:

- market and business models – keeping track of the way the market is changing and the way business needs to alter to keep pace;
- business processes – the way in which value is delivered to clients;
- organisation structure and culture – the way the firm is organised and the culture of how the firm operates;
- technology infrastructure.

Successful change seems to require a series of factors. These are:

- management buy-in and ownership;
- effective project management;
- action to attract and keep the right staff;
- employee ownership of change.

Figure 8.1 illustrates this.

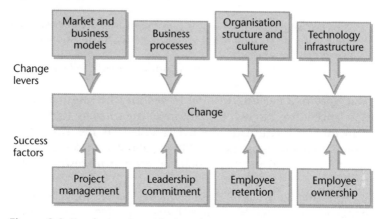

Figure 8.1 Key factors in achieving change

© Chaffey, D. (2002) *E-Business and E-Commerce Management,* Pearson Education Limited. Reprinted by permission of Pearson Education Limited.

We have already looked in depth at most of the change levers. Market and business models were considered as part of the e-business strategy and also when we looked at e-marketing. Businesses processes were analysed in depth as part of the e-business design. We shall now look at how to implement new processes effectively and at technology infrastructure as part of the e-business implementation. What we shall analyse in this chapter is the way in which people can be engaged and enrolled in making things happen.

Organisation structure and culture

These are two very large management topics which are well covered in other texts[1] and can only be touched on here.

Websites have often been standalone areas of marketing activity and as such little attempt has been made to integrate them into the overall operation of the firm. This often happens by default since the website is 'out there' and does not appear to have much impact on the day-to-day workings of the firm apart from a few extra e-mails in the inbox.

There is much debate about whether e-business operations ought to be standalone enterprises. For example, if you operate an online conveyancing service, should you set this up as a separate unit or even business? The general feeling is that it is better to integrate the Internet into your overall business activities rather than to create a separate entity. This has been the thrust of this book and the CBI recently reported that most small and medium enterprises (SMEs) are adopting this approach.

However, as in the first couple of years of getting it all up and running, a project management approach is the best one, where a project board is set up to manage the defining and implementation of the e-business infrastructure. This can then turn into an editorial panel to manage the website once it has been set up. The focus then changes from getting infrastructure and design implemented to managing the structure and content, making sure that both keep pace with market demands, and what clients are saying.

Setting up a project board is discussed in more detail in Chapter 6 on implementation.

Inevitably there will be tensions between setting time aside to manage in this way and fee earning work. There are no easy solutions to this, particularly if you don't have dedicated members of staff for either practice management or IT. The bottom line is that effective e-business activity – like any activity – requires effective management and that takes time. Unfortunately e-business is not a magic bullet, but don't forget that it can also be fun to explore new pastures and think about new possibilities. There are genuine opportunities here to remake legal business.

Types of organisation culture

There is wealth of business literature on the topic of organisation culture. Gurus such as Charles Handy[2] have written whole books about it and Mayson (1997)[3] also dedicates a section to discussing it. There are various diagnostic frameworks to help you work out what sort of culture your firm is operating. The point is that certain cultures have characteristics that make change harder.

So what is organisation culture? The simplest way to put it is the way things get done in the firm. Of course diagnosing the type of culture you have is very different from changing it. A simple diagnostic model is:[4]

- *Survival (outward looking, flexible)* – the external environment plays a significant role in governing firm strategy. The firm will be driven by customer demands and will be an innovator. It may have a relatively flat management structure.
- *Productivity (outward looking, ordered)* – interfaces with the external environment are well structured and the firm is typically fees-driven and is likely to have a hierarchical structure.
- *Human relations (inward looking, flexible)* – this is the organisation as family, with interpersonal relationships more important than reporting channels. A flatter structure and staff development and empowerment are regarded as important by partners.
- *Stability (inward looking, ordered)* – the environment is essentially ignored with managers concentrating on internal efficiency managed through a hierarchical structure.

Which culture is best for e-business?

The *survival* culture will be one that thrives on chaos and fits well with the dynamic e-business environment. However, with relatively little focus on internal systems there could be problems with keeping web content updated and responding to clients' requests from the website. Staff are very responsive to change.

The *productivity* culture is arguably the best one to meet the requirements of e-business. It is client focused yet orderly. The hierarchical structure may make it less flexible to responding to client demands and decision making and implementation may be slow. Staff are less responsive to change.

Human relations culture – this type of firm is well placed to communicate effectively with clients and understand their needs from e-business. The lack of well defined control may cause problems. Staff are responsive to change.

Finally, *stability*. This type of organisation will be slow to respond to the e-business challenge, perhaps waiting for others to test the water. Once it does decide to act it ought to be able to implement e-business quite well. Staff will be very unresponsive to change.

This kind of analysis may help you understand what the

appetite for change is in your firm (see Chapter 4 on e-business strategy).

Changing the organisation culture

How do you realign your culture to one that is maybe more suitable for e-business? This is not an insignificant task and involves a whole range of thinking and activities well beyond the scope of this book. However, as Mayson[5] points out, different areas of your firm may already have different cultures depending on the nature of their work. One approach may be to start with one area of your firm and work on generating that as an e-business oriented group rather than trying to change the whole firm. If this group achieves success then it is likely that the rest of the firm may be more inclined to follow suit.

Many firms are already experimenting with these kinds of approaches by setting up different units to handle different types of work in different ways. For example, some firms now have a team approach to conveyancing, with a dedicated team for re-mortgaging and another for domestic sales. They have adopted approaches found in other industries like call centres to handle enquiries and are continually experimenting with the qualified/unqualified mix of staff to achieve maximum cost effectiveness. Other firms are experimenting with home working, job sharing and various other methods of flexible working to encourage and promote a healthier life/work balance.

These are all things that are changing organisation culture. The key point is to be aware of the culture in which you are operating and think about how this may help or hinder the changes you want to make.

Changing business processes

We looked at redesigning business processes in Chapter 4 on e-business design and also in Chapter 6 on implementation. Business processes are the primary change lever for e-business.

At a more micro level, changing business processes will also change the organisation culture. The topic of business processes comes up again and again in the context of e-business. This is not surprising since it is the way of doing things – the business process – that is fundamentally impacted by the Internet.

Business processes comprise a mixture of electronic and manual tasks. How these two elements fit together in the day-to-day working context is where changes will occur. It is likely that some manual tasks will now be based on the Internet, with other tasks disappearing altogether. Tasks that used to be done on back-office systems may now also be done on the Internet, either on the website or as the result of some other process taking place, for example, a client e-mailing a request via the client extranet, where once they would have picked up the telephone.

There is no quick and simple answer to designing and adopting new business processes. It is very much a case of trial and error and patience is the key. It becomes very easy to blame the system and lose motivation when things go wrong. Wishing for a return to the old days when it could all be done on a typewriter and there was still time to close for lunch can be very tempting. The thing not to do is pretend it's business as usual and put pressure on staff to instantly perform at the same level. Of course the intention is that the change will be of positive benefit, but it will take time to settle. Impatience is one of the key pitfalls of IT implementation and there have been many 'without prejudice' letters fired off to vendors because of it, a reaction which tends to slow things down even further as the vendor runs for cover – certainly not the outcome the firm intended.

The best way to change business processes is to implement them as part of the overall IT infrastructure. This means that everyone gets trained not just in how the IT part of the new system works, but attention is also paid to how the manual processes interact with it. Training design is very important (see below).

Project management

Project management has already been mentioned in Chapter 6 on implementation and overall control of the project will reside with a project board (see above). However, the issue of who will be the project manager, that is the person who is accountable to the board day-to-day for getting the project done, is important. As was mentioned in Chapter 6 the problem is who owns and controls the resources. Many firms look to their IT vendor to manage the implementation process for them, but the project manager they appoint does not have the authority to commit internal resources to the project.

Many specialist legal IT vendors have become experts in this field over the years as they have implemented large numbers of practice and case management systems in a wide range of firms. Most now allocate a dedicated project manager to oversee implementation who works in conjunction with a specific person in the firm who has been given the authority to allocate internal resources. It is essential that you participate fully with your IT vendor and work with them as a business partner rather than as a 'mere supplier'.

Some firms also employ independent specialist project managers who design, plan and then manage the project and all the resources and who has no axe to grind with anyone. This approach works best for large projects where there may be a number of external players as well as the involvement of internal staff. This is one way to diffuse competing commercial interests.

It goes without saying that staff who are working to help set up the e-business cannot also be spending time fee earning or supporting fee earners. This is an obvious point but one that is not well understood. It does not work to ask secretaries to participate in designing and helping build e-business projects, if, at the end of the day, they find their in-trays piled high with tapes that they are still expected to type.

Leadership commitment

Getting partnership commitment to change is possibly one of the hardest things facing a firm, yet all research shows that a key factor in getting change to work is that leadership, and not just lip service, is shown by senior management. In a law firm context this means that everyone needs to see that the senior and managing partners are behind the project and taking an active interest in it, to the extent of actually using the technology they are advocating. The rest of the partnership also needs to buy into it and provide leadership in their own departments. But this is not as easy as it seems. Often there can be frustration in a firm due to the different levels of IT understanding and literacy amongst partners and staff. A question that is often asked is what to do about technophobic partners. How can you persuade/cajole/convince them that this is worth taking on? There are various approaches which hinge on showing and providing benefits to them personally as well as to the firm. It also depends on who is trying to do the persuading. At the risk of sounding trite, here are some tactics that firms have tried:

- *The 'it's good to talk' approach* – actively and regularly canvassing and listening to their concerns. It's amazing how often people jump to permanent conclusions about what other people think because of a single incident in the past. Just because one conversation went a certain way it does not mean it will go that way in the future. The point is to engage in an ongoing dialogue and seek to provide information. This, of course, is as true about clients as it is about partners. The temptation is to stop communicating with a person who does not immediately agree with you.

- *The 'what's in it for them' approach* – spend some time really thinking about the personal benefits that are available for them as well as the benefits for the firm. Speak to them about these. What are their 'hot buttons', i.e. what are they interested in? What are their 'negative hot buttons', i.e. what turns them off? These can be both personal and organisational. For example, a senior partner may have day-to-day concerns associated with current responsibilities and feel that taking on IT is a bridge too far. They may also be reluctant to admit that they don't know how to operate a computer, or feel stupid that they don't know how to surf the Internet. Think about what counts as good news for them and play to this.

- *The 'stick and carrot' approach* – providing a briefing to all partners on the impact of IT and e-business on legal business, and in particular what the threats to the business are. This, of course, is followed up by the opportunities.

- *The 'training and empowerment' approach* – providing one-on-one training or coaching on using a PC. Sometimes the block is that people feel threatened because they can't use the technology effectively or maybe at all. The sense of personal empowerment can work wonders.

- *The 'get your CPD points at any price' approach* – encouraging them to attend seminars designed to educate fee earners on the benefits of the Internet and e-business. Most of these seminars accrue CPD points. Of course, if the partner has no interest in such topics then they are unlikely to allocate precious fee earning time to leaving the office. The trick is to create a context in which this kind of thing becomes instantly more interesting, for example by pointing out what a competitor is doing in their specific field and how you might lose (or gain) business.

- *The 'client' approach* – imagining your partner to be a client who you had to make understand some particularly unpalatable piece of news and who then had to make an important decision. How would you approach this? Maybe your assumptions would be different. This shift in assumptions may make the difference to communicating effectively with the person in question.

Employee ownership

This is probably the most important topic for change in general and e-business in particular. The Case Study describes one way not to go about achieving it.

CASE STUDY   **A tale of two word processors**

I was once called into a firm where it appeared that some of the support staff had suffered a massive loss in productivity. The way it was described was the equivalent of a corporate heart attack. Productivity had just collapsed and was not responding to resuscitation. So what had happened? On the surface it was a simple case of switching from WordPerfect in DOS to Word in Windows. But how it had been done was not helpful.

The secretaries had been encouraged to take a week's holiday at the same time. While they were away their PCs were replaced with Windows based machines with Word rather than WordPerfect. When they got back from their holidays and switched their computers on, they found that the world in which they worked had completely changed. No one had said anything to them about this intended change. There was no offer of training and they sat there puzzled and confused. They had no idea how to use a mouse until rather belatedly some training was provided.

You can imagine the resistance to learning about the new software. The owners of the firm wanted confirmation of what Word was capable of, since every time they asked the secretaries to do

> something they said Word couldn't do it – and the partners had no
> way of knowing one way or the other.
>   Eventually the situation got sorted out and productivity
> revived, in no small part because the secretaries were fundamentally
> committed to doing a good job and stuck with it. It had genuinely
> never occurred to the partners that this was not the way to effect
> change.

The strategic significance of e-business needs to be clearly communicated to staff. The reason for this is that e-business will have a major impact on the way they work. There will be disruption to their work as the new system and work practices are introduced.

There may well be resistance to change. This tends to follow a set pattern which has been described by Adams et al. (1976)[6] and is known as the 'change curve'. See Figure 8.2.

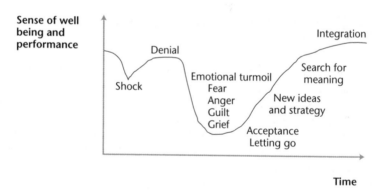

Figure 8.2 The change curve

If staff have not been enrolled in the changes then what usually happens is that they will try and project blame onto the system and will identify major faults where only minor bugs exist. This damages the reputation of the system and a downward spiral begins. The more people think the system is wrong and can't perform its functions, the more minor issues seem to become major faults.

Another issue is avoidance of the system. Here staff will work around it, continuing to do their tasks in their old ways. If you're not watching out for this, it may well seem that the system is a failure. What usually happens next is the vendor gets blamed. This sets off another downward spiral as the vendor loses faith in you as a customer (and this really does happen). Things go from bad to worse. The partner in charge of the system becomes stressed and the partnership gets upset and starts demanding recompense from the vendor. And so on and so on. The key is to get staff willing the system to work rather than fail.

Achieving organisational change

Schein (1992)[7] suggests a model for achieving organisational change that involves three stages:

1. Unfreeze the present position by creating a climate of change through education, training and motivation of future participants.
2. Quickly move from the present situation to the new desired state.
3. Refreeze by making the system an accepted part of the way the organisation operates.

To achieve the unfreezing stage, different members of staff can be identified for different roles by the project manager:

- *system sponsors* are the partners and other senior managers in the firm who have bought into the e-business initiative. They are committed to major change and want it to be a success. They will try and fire up staff with their enthusiasm and stress why the system is important to the business and its workers.
- *system owners* are managers of the key processes such as the practice manager or the partner in charge of the particular area where the new system is to be focused.
- *system users* are the people who are actively involved in making the process happen.

Special types of systems users can be identified, and it is impor-tant for the project manager to try to influence these members of staff and achieve commitment among other staff. The three main types of users are:

- *Stakeholders*, who should be identified for each of the areas where change will be introduced. These will be staff who are respected by their co-workers and will be enthusiastic about the system. They should be involved in process design workshops, on the project board and involved in the procurement process.
- *Legitimizers*, who are the people who protect the norms and values of the system. They are experienced at their jobs and are regarded as experts by other staff. Initially they may be resistant to change so need to be involved early.
- *Opinion leaders*, whom others watch to see whether they accept the new ideas and changes. They usually have little formal power but are very influential and regarded as good ideas people. They are usually receptive to change and should also be involved in the process.

Creating a climate of change: techniques for working with staff

As outlined above, it makes very good sense to identify the staff in the above roles and involve them from the outset. This is not just to get staff buy-in and acceptance but also to achieve a much better design which works for everyone. A firm that operates in this inclusive way is a much more pleasant place to be in, as people start to focus on making things work rather than on what doesn't work.

Workshops

Staff can be involved in a variety of ways. A particularly useful method is to hold audit and design workshops where staff are encouraged to talk about the things that work and the things that don't with the current systems. They are then asked to design their ideal system and this is worked through at the business process level. This is particularly effective not only for designing new and better ways of working, but also for empowering staff to feel they have had their say. The group process also facilitates some very good solutions to common problems as group brainstorming sessions can be very creative. Finally, any frustrations or things that are beneath the waterline can be identified and tackled in a proactive way.

A good example is a firm where junior support staff aired their views on the way documentation was presented to clients. They were very keen that the firm should present a highly professional image to clients and referrers. They had thought long and hard about the issues and came up with some very simple and cost effective solutions. Their commitment to the firm was obvious and they also clearly appreciated being consulted on things that mattered to them.

In focusing on systems, processes and procedures frustrations about the way things operate can be aired without anyone being blamed. This can be a liberating experience. The key, of course, is to ensure that the workshops are followed up by solid action.

Internal seminars

An allied and similar approach is to hold seminars for staff. This works particularly well for senior fee earners and partners. A seminar can provide not only an opportunity for consultation but also some genuine education. Staff can leave feeling that their time has been well spent because they have learnt something. Seminars can also provide a useful forum for doing collective problem solving. Again focusing on systems, processes and procedures enables people to express the things that are not working without involving personalities.

Training and development

Many IT vendors complain that training is the first thing that gets cut from any proposal in a negotiation to cut costs. The usual way of doing this is to adopt a 'train the trainer' approach where an already hard pressed member of the support staff is trained up with a view to having them train everyone else. This can work – but in reality is a high risk strategy. It is very rare that the particular member of support staff is taken off regular duties to concentrate on the new role. The other issue is that training skill is not simply a function of knowing how to use the system. A good trainer also has to be able to communicate effectively, have a great deal of patience and credibility with the trainees.

The issues around training go far deeper than simply providing hands-on training for people using the system. The all important thing is the context within which the training is provided. It is too easy to see training as a necessary evil to get the system up and running – rather like feeding the dragon to keep it quiet. A much more empowering approach is to define training inside the context of the ongoing development of staff members. The particular training provided may look exactly the same, but the attitude of the trainee and hence their willingness to learn will be very different. This human centred approach is vital for success in e-business. Staff who feel taken care of tend to provide good service to clients.

Staff surfing the Internet

Encourage your staff to surf the Internet and check out what the competition is doing. Provide them with the training they need to do this. There is often a fear that staff are surfing the Net in the firm's time and many firms ask about how they can limit staff access to the Internet. This is certainly possible. However, think about it. If you are serious about developing an e-business and then seek to limit the way staff use the Internet there is a mixed message here. It also sends out the message that you don't trust your staff. This is a question about management rather than Internet usage. It is far better to allow staff to surf within clear guidelines and to encourage feedback on any good ideas they come across.

Policies for use of e-mail and the Internet

It is important to have clear policies and guidelines for the use of the Internet. For example, the firm should be clear about the nature of material it will not allow to be downloaded onto its systems. There should also be a clear policy on e-mail use. There are many excellent resources on the web on e-mail usage, for example **www.email-policy.com**.

Other techniques

Other techniques to include staff in the change process include:

- seeking views by questionnaires (and remembering to publish the results so everyone can see the outcome);

- having monthly updates for all staff – either in staff meetings or by e-mail.

Conclusion

Managing the people issues around IT and e-business is probably of greater importance than selecting and implementing the right hardware and software. People are ingenious and can achieve a lot with very little if they are clear about the vision and enthusiastic about what is possible. If they are given the right opportunities to participate, particularly if they are consulted about changes and are trained to make those changes, then any project is likely to be a success, even if there are technical difficulties. It almost goes without saying that if they are not, then even the best hardware and software in the world will not deliver the intended result. People are key.

Notes

1   Mayson, S. (1997) *Making Sense of Law Firms*, Blackstone, London.
2   Handy, C. (1996) *The Gods of Management*, Oxford University Press.
3   Mayson, *Making Sense of Law Firms* pp. 340 ff.
4   Boddy, D., Boonstra, A. and Kennedy, G. (2001) *Managing the Information Revolution*, Pearson Education, Harlow.
5   Mayson, *Making Sense of Law Firms*.
6   Adams, J., Hayes, J. and Hopson, B. (1976) *Transitions: Understanding and managing personal change*, Martin Robertson, London.
7   Schein, E. (1992) *Organisational Culture and Leadership*, Jossey Bass, San Francisco CA.

Conclusion

This book has been about web-enabling legal practice with a view to developing and delivering good client service and care. It should have encouraged you to think beyond 'having a website' to really taking a look at what the Internet and Internet technologies make available, particularly the opportunity to innovate and enhance the way you design and deliver legal service. The suggested approach for this is to look at the way you currently do things (your business processes) and actively work out ways in which the Internet and its technologies can bring real benefit to your clients and in return real business benefit to your firm. The importance of encapsulating this in a written strategy and business case is emphasised. We have covered the pitfalls of becoming technology driven rather than service driven and the issues around choosing a vendor and implementing an e-business system. Finally, we looked at the importance of making sure all the people involved in the process are engaged and managed effectively.

But what should you do now? It has been said that commentating on the Internet is like trying to predict the outcome of a 24-hour poker game after the first five minutes. Predicting what the future holds for law firms and the Internet is a similarly impossible task. However, here are some trends that might indicate that you should seriously consider web-enabling part or all of your legal practice:

- The regulatory framework, particularly around electronic signatures and authentication of documents, is agreed – resulting in more and more paperwork (for example around financial services) being completed online.
- The web becomes a common delivery medium for local and national government. For example, payments for London's traffic congestion charge are now being taken online. Look out for the web becoming more and more integrated into government administration.

- Broadband (XDSL) (and faster methods of communication) becomes the normal method of Internet connection for everyone, including homes.
- Mobile phones, PDAs and laptops converge even further into one fully connected handheld device that has fast connection to the Internet.
- Standard software in common use becomes fully web-enabled – that is, it assumes that the Internet will be a routine part of how things get done (Microsoft has its dot Net strategy already in progress). This is likely to encourage web-enablement when you next upgrade your industry standard software.

The trend towards web-enablement is also being driven by the legal agencies, most of which see cost savings through the effective use of the Internet as a delivery and collection medium. The Legal Services Commission and Land Registry are already demonstrating this and it is highly likely that all the other legal agencies will follow suit, looking for ways to achieve cost savings and increased efficiency through encouraging their users to interact with them electronically.

The one inescapable conclusion is that the twenty-first century is web-enabled and law firms will need to keep pace to survive and prosper.

Bibliography

Amor, D. (2000) *The E-Business (R)evolution*, Prentice Hall.

Barnes, S. and Hunt, B. (2000) *E-Commerce and V-Business*, Butterworth-Heinemann.

Bayles, D. (1997) *Extranets*, Prentice Hall.

Bickerton, P. et al (2000) *Cybermarketing*, Butterworth-Heinemann.

Cairncross, F. (2002) *The Company of the Future*, Profile.

Cassidy, J. (2002) *Dot Con: The Greatest Story Ever Sold*, Penguin.

Chaffey, D. (2001) *E-business and E-commerce Management*, Pearson.

Chen, S. (2001) *Strategic Management of e-Business*, John Wiley.

Christian, C. (1998) *Legal Practice in the Digital Age*, Bowerdean.

Cunningham, M. (2000) *B2B: The Path to Profit*, Pearson.

Cunningham, M. (2002) *Smart Things to Know About E-Business*, Capstone.

Davenport, T. and Prusak, L. (2000) *Working Knowledge*, Harvard.

Dyson, E. (1997) *Release 2.0: A Design for Living in the Digital Age*, Penguin.

Earle, N. and Keen, P. (2000) *From .com to .profit*, Jossey-Bass.

Fellenstein, C. and Wood, R. (2000) *Exploring E-commerce, Global E-business and E-society*, Prentice Hall.

Gates, B. (1996) *The Road Ahead*, Penguin.

Gates, B. (2001) *Business at the Speed of Thought*, Penguin.

Gilligan, C., Lowe, R. and Williamson, A. (1994) *Marketing for Law Firms*, EMIS Professional Publishing.

Gremier, R. and Metes, G. (1995) *Going Virtual*, Prentice Hall.

Hammond, R. (1996) *Digital Business*, Hodder and Stoughton.

Kalakota, R. and Robinson, M. (2000) *E-Business 2.0: Roadmap for Success*, Addison Wesley.

Levine, R. et al (2000) *The Cluetrain Manifesto*, Pearson.

May, P. (2000) *The Business of E-Commerce*, CUP.

Middleton, J. (2000) *Writing the New Economy*, Capstone.

Papows, J. (1999) *Enterprise.com*, Nicholas Brealey.

Phillips, N. (2001) *E-motional Business*, Pearson.

Salter, B. et al (2000) *The Complete Idiots Guide to E-Commerce UK*, Pearson.

Siegel, D. (1999) *Futurize your Enterprise*, John Wiley.

Sleight, S. (2001) *Essential Managers: Moving to E-Business*, Dorling Kindersley.

Smith, P. and Chaffey, D. (2002) *E-marketing excellence*, Butterworth-Heinemann.

Susskind, R. (2000) *Transforming the Law*, OUP.

Susskind, R. (1996) *The Future of Law*, OUP.

Tapscott, D. and McQueen, R. (1995) *Digital Economy*, McGraw-Hill.

Tapscott D. and Caston, A. (1992) *Paradigm Shift*, McGraw-Hill.

Terrett, A. (2000) *The Internet: Business Strategies for Law Firms*, Law Society Publishing.

Tiwana, A. (2001) *The Essential Guide to Knowledge Management*, Prentice Hall.

Wallace, J. (1997) *Overdrive*, John Wiley.

Index